"Christian parents urgently ne[...]
agers through the white-water [...]
Andrew and Christian Walker know what they are talking about, and they
are both sweet Christian parents and faithful Christian thinkers. They are
brilliantly insightful, and this book is perfectly timed."

R. Albert Mohler Jr., President, The Southern Baptist Theological
Seminary

"Our team at Focus on the Family is seeing an increasingly common theme
in the calls and correspondence we receive: Christian parents are deeply
concerned about the culture and its impact on their kids. These moms and
dads are looking for help discussing tough topics with their children, which
is why I'm so encouraged that Andrew and Christian Walker have released
this timely and engaging book, *What Do I Say When . . . ?* I'm confident
many parents will refer to this volume often as they point their kids toward
the Bible's teaching on challenging issues."

Jim Daly, President, Focus on the Family

"Andrew and Christian Walker provide an incredibly rich and deeply practical resource for Christian parents in their book *What Do I Say When . . . ?*
The Walkers are a perfect pair to pen such a resource with their educational
and vocational backgrounds, as well as their intentionality with parenting.
They have dug deep into Scripture and brought forth a timely resource for
parents navigating the current chaos in our culture. I encourage parents to
pick up this resource and enjoy!"

Lauren McAfee, Ministry Director, Hobby Lobby Ministry
Investments; Founder, Stand for Life; coauthor, *Beyond Our Control*

"This is a rare book that is practical, wise, robustly theological, and usable at
the dinner table. Andrew and Christian Walker have given a profound gift
to those of us parenting in this chaotic cultural moment. And the stories
are the best part, especially for those of us who don't always know how to
get a conversation started with our children."

John Stonestreet, President, Colson Center; coauthor, *A Practical
Guide to Culture*

"As a mom to two young kids, this book is exactly what I need to navigate tough, cultural conversations from a biblical worldview. It's more important than ever to be confident in the theological and biblical truth behind *why* we believe what we do when explaining things to our kids. Kids today want answers they can stand on. This book delivers."

Ericka Andersen, author, *Reason to Return: Why Women Need the Church and the Church Needs Women*

"*What Do I Say When . . . ?* is a needed book for all pastors who are looking for biblical, gospel-centered, and practical resources to equip their church. I plan to order a box to give to the parents in our church to help them disciple their children in these challenging times. The book is faithful to God's word and easy to implement. My wife and I have already used it in our own parenting."

Jason Dees, Senior Pastor, Christ Covenant, Atlanta, Georgia

"What a truly helpful and delightfully practical book! In a culture of chaos, it's more important than ever that Christians know how to discuss difficult topics with their kids in a way that is faithful to the truth of Scripture. The Walkers have provided an outstanding resource that will give you the biblical clarity and confidence you need to have some of the conversations that matter most today, all in a mercifully short format. *What Do I Say When . . . ?* achieves the perfect balance of depth and accessibility that every busy parent needs."

Natasha Crain, speaker; podcaster; author, *Keeping Your Kids on God's Side*

"Parents often discover, to their dismay, that their children are asking difficult questions about thorny issues that they didn't even realize existed. Christian parents need trusted voices to help them apply biblical truths and godly wisdom to the ethical confusion and cultural insanity that the world relentlessly throws at their kids. Thank God that Andrew and Christian Walker have written an indispensable guide for families to face the hard things head-on with a confidence that the Bible is sufficient to navigate the troubled waters of twenty-first-century chaos. This book is a lifeline for drowning parents!"

Hershael W. York, Victor and Louise Lester Professor of Christian Preaching and Dean of the School of Theology, The Southern Baptist Theological Seminary

"As a pastor I love this book, and as a dad I'm thrilled. If churches and parents won't disciple their children, the world will, and the Walkers have given us a center-bullseye resource to apply the lordship of Christ to the chaos of our kids' culture."

Josh Howerton, Senior Pastor, Lakepointe Church, Rockwall, Texas

What Do I Say When . . . ?

What Do I Say When . . . ?

A Parents' Guide to Navigating Cultural
Chaos for Children and Teens

Andrew T. Walker and Christian Walker

WHEATON, ILLINOIS

What Do I Say When . . . ? A Parents' Guide to Navigating Cultural Chaos for Children and Teens

© 2024 by Andrew T. Walker and Christian Walker

Published by Crossway
        1300 Crescent Street
        Wheaton, Illinois 60187

Published in association with the literary agency of Wolegmuth & Associates, Inc.

Cover design: Faceout Studio

First printing 2024

Printed in the United States of America

Scripture quotations are from the ESV® Bible (The Holy Bible, English Standard Version®), © 2001 by Crossway, a publishing ministry of Good News Publishers. Used by permission. All rights reserved. The ESV text may not be quoted in any publication made available to the public by a Creative Commons license. The ESV may not be translated in whole or in part into any other language.

All emphases in Scripture quotations have been added by the authors.

Trade paperback ISBN: 978-1-4335-9274-4
ePub ISBN: 978-1-4335-9276-8
PDF ISBN: 978-1-4335-9275-1

Library of Congress Cataloging-in-Publication Data

Names: Walker, Andrew T., 1985- author. | Walker, Christian, 1985- author.
Title: What do I say when . . . ? : a parent's guide to navigating cultural chaos for children and teens / Andrew T. Walker and Christian Walker.
Description: Wheaton, Illinois : Crossway, [2024] | Includes bibliographical references and index.
Identifiers: LCCN 2024003236 (print) | LCCN 2024003237 (ebook) | ISBN 9781433592744 (Trade paperback) | ISBN 9781433592751 (PDF) | ISBN 9781433592768 (ePub)
Subjects: LCSH: Parenting—Religious aspects—Christianity. | Parent and child—Religious aspects—Christianity. | Christian youth—Conduct of life.
Classification: LCC BV4529 .W2555 2024 (print) | LCC BV4529 (ebook) | DDC 248.8/45—dc23/eng/20240422
LC record available at https://lccn.loc.gov/2024003236
LC ebook record available at https://lccn.loc.gov/2024003237

Crossway is a publishing ministry of Good News Publishers.

VP   33   32   31   30   29   28   27   26   25   24
15   14   13   12   11   10   9   8   7   6   5   4   3   2   1

We dedicate this book to our daughters,
Caroline, Catherine, and Charlotte.

You each bring us more joy than you can ever possibly understand.

Contents

Acknowledgments

EVERY BOOK IS a labor of time, love, and frustration. What thing worth doing in life isn't?

We want to say thank you to a number of people who supported us in the drafting of this book. We want to thank our agent Andrew Wolgemuth for all of his help in overseeing the development of this book from start to finish. Champ Thornton at Crossway has been nothing but a cheerful encouragement to us. We also want to thank friends who reviewed the manuscript and provided us with feedback: Whitney Bruce, Dean Inserra, Carey Murphy, Morgan Nichter, and Erik Reed. And of course, our own moms and dads (Fred and Sue Walker and Duncan and Lynda Locke) for their pursuit of having their children in church every Sunday and Wednesday when it would have been convenient to do otherwise.

Introduction

WE ARE LIVING IN a moment of rapid cultural change that is leaving everyday Christians and Christian parents completely flat-footed. Change is not new, of course, but historians could point to recent developments in the culture that signal how fast that change is happening, compared to past times.

As I (Andrew) speak across the United States, one of the most frequently asked questions I get is: "How do Christian parents equip their children to face the cultural challenges in front of them? And how do you do it in age-appropriate ways?"

One of the answers I always give goes like this:

You must catechize and disciple your children at ever-younger ages intentionally, or else the culture will do so unintentionally and with even greater effectiveness.

If you don't teach your children, the world will.

Moreover, if you think two hours per week in church and the well-intentioned efforts of your youth pastor excuse you from having to talk about these topics (some of them *very* awkward), then I regret to inform you that your outlook needs to change.

In response, heads always nod, and low-murmured voices give near-unanimous affirmation to my answer. What I say out loud, all parents seem to internally recognize themselves. But that raises the important question: What are the topics needing to be discussed, and what's the best way to discuss them?

That is what this book intends to offer to weary parents: a resource to equip you to equip your children. If you aren't discipling your children, we can be sure that secular classrooms, peer groups, and social media will.

It is really difficult to be parents in today's culture. We feel this ourselves. Actually, every parent in every culture in every generation has probably had to face difficulties of their own and said the same thing. But today's culture seems to be moving at such a fast rate that it feels impossible to keep up with what's happening. It's difficult to stay on top of discipling our children to understand and rely on God's word. We hope and pray that we are discipling our children to use their knowledge of Scripture to stand firm against the war Satan is waging through mass cultural confusion.

It's all happening so fast that I (Christian) often feel left in the dust. Andrew will ask me often, "Did you hear x, y, z today on the news?" My response is usually, "No. I've been teaching since 7:00 a.m., helping our children with homework, cooking dinner, switching over laundry, and now we're putting kids to bed. When would I have had time to hear that?" He laughs and says, "I forget that you don't live in my world. It's amazing how our attentions can be so focused on different things." Not everyone lives in Andrew's world. He knows everything about everything almost exactly as it happens. He is an expert on culture and current events. And yet I live in the same house, literally sleep in the same bed, and cannot keep up. I've tried to become an expert by osmosis, but I never feel as though I measure up.

I (Christian) need help. I want to do my best, but I am busy, tired, and don't know how to make the sun stay up and give me more time during the day (see Josh. 10:12–14). Does anyone else feel that way? I am no expert on today's constantly shifting culture, but I desperately want to help my children plant the Lord's word deep in their hearts, understand what's facing them in the culture today, and know how to stand against it both with God's love and truth. I wanted to be a part of writing this book so that I could have it for myself to use in my own home with my own children.

Let's be clear: this is not a parenting book from authors who have parenting all figured out. In fact, we are emphatic in telling friends that we are not writing a parenting book but a book for parents. The subtle difference is important: we haven't mastered the art of parenting. What we offer is a unique combination of expertise in thinking about what the Bible says about current issues facing Christians and how to translate those answers for everyday Christian parents to use conversationally with their children.

We are writing this book because we also need this book in our own home just as much as we want you to have this book in your home. We are parents of three young girls who ask us questions daily. We are parents who strive to lead our children to understand the way God created the universe and the way we fit into his world. We are parents who eagerly pray for their salvation. We need help with all of those things too!

So, if we as parents need this book too, what makes us think we're qualified to write it? We're only able to do this together! I (Andrew) teach Christian ethics at the Southern Baptist Theological

Seminary in Louisville, Kentucky. Therefore, I write, speak, and teach on cultural issues facing Christians, including some of today's most controversial topics, regularly. My experience has allowed me to help parents understand the ethical issues at hand and understand how God intended for us to interpret these issues according to his twofold revelation in (1) his revealed word that we call Scripture and (2) his revelation in nature and creation order. I (Christian) am a children's curriculum writer and educator in both children's ministry and elementary education settings. My experience has allowed me to understand how children learn best, and I've developed my abilities to communicate gospel truths to little hearts in developmentally and age-appropriate ways.

Accessible, Trustworthy, and Age-Appropriate

We want this resource to be accessible, trustworthy, and age-appropriate. First of all, busy parents need this book to be accessible. As busy parents ourselves, we know too well the difficulty of finding time to read lengthy books and process the material to disciple our children. We desire for this book to be a quick reference guide, a short and readable book for you to use to help guide the discipleship of your children.

Second, we pray that this book is trustworthy. We prayed over this book for months before beginning to write it. We asked the Lord to guide our words directly from his Scripture. These are not our thoughts about today's culture. God has revealed himself in his word and in the natural order of his creation. He had a plan from the beginning of his creation for all of creation. We learn of that plan in his word. We will be using his word and his good plan to define our responses to today's cultural issues. And it's good to remember that as uncharted as culture seems today, these are not new ideas that the church is facing. The church has been facing these issues for centuries in some manner.

Lastly, we are writing this book to be age-appropriate. Certain ages can handle certain levels of understanding and comprehension of topics. As we said previously, it's difficult as busy parents to discern what levels of understanding are appropriate for our children after reading a lengthy book on a heavy topic. We want to help take the guesswork out of the way for you. Each cultural topic will be intentionally broken down into developmentally appropriate and age-appropriate levels of understanding for your children. Hopefully, this will help guide you in discipling your family in the most helpful and effective ways possible.

In this book, we have devoted ten chapters to ten important cultural topics facing children and families today. Not every topic that could be discussed is discussed, sadly. To do that, a much longer book would be necessary. But our goal for this book is to provide the essentials, not the last word on every subject. These chapters are quick reference guides that give the very basic foundations and introductions to these cultural topics. There is so much more to say and so much more to learn, but we wanted to give you the very basics to help you begin teaching and discipling your children.

Each chapter begins by introducing the topic. We then explain what God says about that topic and what should be laid as the biblical foundation for parents to understand. From there, each chapter moves into a portion for parents to use as a guide for talking with their children about the cultural topic. Because we believe the home is central to the development of the next

Christian generation, we're calling our sequence of conversational instruction "floors" that correspond to a home. Each chapter has three "floors" of biblical truths and conversation starters. Instead of having strict age guidelines, we are using "floors" to help guide you to determine where your child may best fit based on development, maturity, and age.

First-floor children are probably between the ages of four and eight, second-floor children are probably between the ages of eight and twelve, and third-floor children are probably between twelve and sixteen. If you think your child is ready for a more mature conversation, then move up to the next floor. If you think your child is not ready for a conversation, then move down to the floor below. The floors are not rigid and are intended to guide you in discussing the topics thoroughly as your child grows and help you to keep ahead of culture.

Remember that you want to be the first person to have the conversation with your child to be able to lay the biblical foundation. Otherwise, culture will form the foundation for you. Stay vigilant and keep ahead of culture.

Both a Defensive and Offensive Resource

We pray that this book will be used as a defensive and offensive resource.

I (Christian) need a quick reference defensive tool. When I drive home from school with the girls, there is so much chatter in the car: stories from the school day, observations of flags and signs in people's yards, and talk about movies and songs. All the chatter leads to questions about what things mean, the definition of new words, how people interact with each other, and so forth.

I am hit fast and furious with questions I need to answer and comments that I have to patrol for the various ages and levels of maturity of my daughters as I drive. I need answers to these questions. Some answers I have, sometimes I have no idea what to say, and other times I need help finding where to look in Scripture. Additionally for all of these responses, I need help figuring out how to answer them in age-appropriate ways for all three of our girls. If they all heard the same thing in the car, then they all need a solid, biblical answer. I need this book! I am going to find the corresponding cultural topics, quickly read the short chapter, then find the floor response for each child. I can defensively disciple the girls with biblical truths as they come to me with questions.

A Proactive Tool

We also pray that this book is used as a proactive tool. We hope to use this book as a family devotional tool. Each chapter includes one unifying Scripture verse that ties all of the biblical truths together. We want our entire family to memorize the verse as we learn about the cultural topic together. We use the biblical truths and conversation starters to guide our family devotional time. Maybe your family needs to focus on one chapter for a while because you're facing something specific. Perhaps you are about to encounter a gay family member at a family event and need to equip your children. Maybe your family would like to move through the book chapter by chapter. Just remember that you are the one who needs to lay the biblical foundation with your children.

Biblical truths could be referenced and recited for memory and mastery. Discussion starters could be used to check in on your children's understanding or growing knowledge of a topic. There can be check-ins often to see if they have matured and need to begin deepening their biblical understanding by moving to the next "floor."

We want to offer one word about the types of arguments you're going to hear in this book. First, you must realize that if you want your children to survive with their faith intact in our present culture, it's going to require some level of study for both you and your children. Discipleship in today's culture requires a high degree of responsibility. We are, after all, no longer in a culture that just agrees with what Christians believe. A lot of Christian parenting literature does not make complete arguments. What Christian parenting books frequently do is make statements that the author just expects you to agree with. That's fine, but it's also incomplete. Some of the content you're going to read in our book may appear difficult or complex at first. We've tried to make complex arguments as simple as possible, but even then, you're going to have to dig in, read, ponder, and maybe even re-read if something is not immediately clear. That's inevitable when wading through difficult subjects. Issues in this book are not as much complex as they are simply controversial given the culture we live in. But let us encourage you: there is no greater investment of your time, focus, and energy than effort put forward on behalf of your children to build up their faith in order to thrive in our culture. You can do this.

One thing that we pray you remember is that God has given your precious children to you to protect and disciple. But he has not given you the power of salvation. Only God can rescue your children from their sin (Rom. 1:16). As parents we can do all of the right things, read all of the right books, send our kids to all of the right schools, have the most perfect family devotions (that's never happened at our house, but maybe in yours!)—but it will never be enough. We cannot save them. We should pray over our children, eagerly teach them his truth, and trust that God will be faithful to finish the good work that he has started (Phil. 1:6). We have a responsibility to train them up in righteousness (Deut. 6:4–7; Prov. 22:6; Eph. 6:4), but only he can call them to salvation (Rom. 8:28–30). Mom and Dad, rest in him. Rest in his faithfulness. Rest in his love for your children, which is greater than even yours.

1

Human Dignity

ONE FALL SATURDAY our family went to run errands and then grabbed lunch afterward. As we were leaving the restaurant, a family was entering the restaurant. Our paths crossing, I noticed in the family was a young boy in a wheelchair with severe disabilities. We could tell the boy caught our young girls' attention (they did not awkwardly stare as much as just notice). When we got to the vehicle but before we drove off, I (Andrew) said to the girls, "Girls, I noticed that you saw that young boy in the wheelchair. How should we treat people who for whatever reason cannot use their legs or whose minds may not function properly?" To my delight, one daughter spoke up and said, "Well, God loves that person and that boy is made in God's image, so we should be kind and help where we can."

Perfect answer. That answer proved to me that it is those small conversations along the way that accumulate into a worldview. For a long time, we had been working to instill a concept in our children's minds that only Christianity can fully hold to—human dignity. We did not do this through assigning them books. We have made the intentional plan to drop in these teachings when opportunities allow in the humdrum of daily life.

Christians cannot overlook the tremendous significance of this teaching. Christianity alone provides the best solution for a coherent reason to value a human person and the necessary authority to confidently guarantee it.

This is an idea that all societies require and that other thought systems or worldviews try (and fail) to develop on their own. Every society is governed by ideals that only Christianity can truly explain and resolve with definitive clarity.

At the heart of all political views, religious traditions, or cultural systems are beliefs, stated or unstated, about the value of the human being. Do human beings have actual moral value? Do humans have rights that actually matter? Or are humans mere carbon and water molecules that gained consciousness by sheer coincidence and blind chance? How does one arrive at the conclusion, a conclusion not subject to the whims of mere human opinion, that human beings bear a unique value and that this value should be recognized in and protected by law? What prevents a government from overpowering its own citizens and dispensing with them at will?

From beliefs about the appalling tragedy of the Holocaust to horror at America's past involvement with slavery, modern society hinges upon beliefs about human beings—that human beings are worthy of protection from threats of abuse, wanton endangerment, and tyranny. The question is: Can non-Christian systems arrive at a position of human dignity on their own that does not end up being arbitrary? For example: Why does modern America assign human dignity regardless of skin color such that racism is considered morally wrong (which it is), but the same modern America overlooks human dignity on the basis of size and development and thus approves of abortion? There's an inconsistency at the root of modern America's dilemma on human dignity. Christianity has no such dilemma.

Generally people don't think that human dignity can exist apart from a profound appreciation for the human being as a special product of God's own making. Even atheists will admit this idea. As one atheist publicly acknowledged, "We may have to accept that the concept of the sanctity of human life is a Judeo-Christian notion which might very easily not survive Judeo-Christian civilization." The same author goes on to observe three options facing the atheist with the idea of human dignity. He writes,

> The first option is to fall into the furnace [admitted despair in having no dignity ethic]. Another is to work furiously to nail down an atheist version of the sanctity of the individual. If that does not work, then there is only one other place to go. Which is back to faith, whether we like it or not.[1]

Governments exist for the sake of protecting and facilitating the ability of human beings to live together without wantonly destroying one another. What any earthly political regime believes about the worth of human beings will impact how its people are treated. The question is not whether there will be a concept of dignity (or indignity) at the heart of our culture; the question is whose concept of dignity reigns supreme.

1 Douglas Murray, "Would Human Life Be Sacred in an Atheist World?," *The Spectator*, April 19, 2014, https://www.spectator.co.uk/article/would-human-life-be-sacred-in-an-atheist-world-.

BIBLICAL TEACHING OVERVIEW

Human dignity. What is it? Dignity refers to the moral worth of a human being simply from existing—not from an attribute based on skin color, cognitive ability, athletic skill, age, height, location, or anything else. The good news of human dignity from the Christian worldview is that it is not parceled out by the sovereign decrees of human government or human opinion. There is nothing you or anyone can do to truly subtract from, or even add to, the dignity that someone possesses. We may think we can subtract dignity when we mock or insult someone. But because Christianity teaches that we do not bestow dignity upon a person (we only recognize it), it is impossible for us to truly take it away. Dignity resides within the person.

Human dignity exists as a result of humanity being made in God's image. Christians arrive at this conclusion about human dignity because of who makes human beings—God. Genesis 1:26–27 declares:

> Then God said, "Let us make man in our image, after our likeness. And let them have dominion over the fish of the sea and over the birds of the heavens and over the livestock and over all the earth and over every creeping thing that creeps on the earth."

> So God created man in his own image,
>> in the image of God he created him;
>> male and female he created them.

Though theologians debate the full meaning of "being made in God's image," what every theologian who honors the Bible as God's word recognizes is that Scripture places a pronounced emphasis on the unique status of human beings compared to the rest of creation. As human beings we are not only existent and animate, we are beings whose faculties resemble God's: we can reason with our minds and relate to one another in love. We can organize our activities to reach preconceived goals.

Human dignity is not a mere social construct, brute fact, or convention arrived at by consensus or whatever majorities deem it to be. To be truly protected from arbitrary human opinion, dignity must be and *is* a divine concept that speaks about the unique status of human beings alongside the rest of God's creation. Because dignity is bestowed by God, it is issued with an unbreakable and unchangeable bond and guarantee. As there is no shadow of change in God, so there is no change in the value that God places on human beings.

There's an internal moral logic to the value that Scripture places on the identity and dignity of human beings. The fact that Scripture calls us to love our neighbor assumes we are to respect our neighbor's existence (Mark 12:30–31). Since Christians believe that dignity is the result of divine action, there is also a divine consequence. If you were asked why human beings have dignity, the answer is simply: "Because they do." That might sound like circular reasoning, but if dignity does not exist as a divinely brute fact of someone's existence, then dignity is something that can be added to and subtracted from based on the change in human opinion. Once that type of logic is introduced, it spells disaster for those whom people might recognize as having, perhaps, less dignity. It's no surprise that the history books are full of episodes of government wanting to get rid of people whose lives are considered a "drain" on society. If dignity is not an absolute property tied to one's existence, whether that person—or group of people—is worth respecting can change from one person to another. Every imaginable human injustice has occurred because one group of human beings failed to respect the equal dignity of the other.

The idea of human dignity is a truly unique and revolutionary concept that Christianity introduced into the world. Before Judeo-Christian thought came to predominate in certain areas of the world, it was difficult to say *why* someone's existence should be respected. Christianity says that people are owed respect, honor, and their existence because God delights in creating humans. So much of what we take for granted as Christians living in today's world is built upon the tradition of human dignity that Christianity brought into the world. If we are to respect the so-called "rights" of other human beings, we do so in confidence that rights are real because human beings have real moral worth and moral aspects of their being that are worthy of protection. For example, the universities, hospitals, and the rule of law that so much of our society hinges upon stems from Christian beliefs about the dignity of the human person: that human beings are rational and thus education is valuable for its own sake, that human beings should be treated with healing compassion, and that human beings deserve equal protection under the law (Luke 6:31).

Human dignity stands as the foundation for Christian opposition to any assault on God's image bearers. Christian opposition to any number of social evils is based on our understanding of human dignity. Because all human beings are what they are—human beings made by God—we do not differentiate what is owed to persons because of their skin color, cognitive ability, medical status, or anything else. Racism is abhorrent because it violates human dignity. Determining value based on skin color is as dumb as it is unjust. Euthanasia is evil because it permits killing people under a false concept of compassion. Mocking the intellectually or physically disabled person is egregious because intellectual ability or physical ability is no measure of why a person matters—a person matters because human existence requires honoring an inherent dignity within each person.

Human dignity supplies Christians with the ability to amicably disagree while respecting the value of all persons. Throughout the Bible, we are commanded to seek peace and to do good to those outside the household of faith (Col. 4:5–6). In other words, a Christian account of human dignity allows us to express disagreement while also affirming the inherent worth of every individual, regardless of whether or not they agree with us. This is not a call to abandon or downplay truth in exchange for placating those who disagree with Christians; it is a call to confidently and unapologetically share the truth in a way befitting the respect that other human beings deserve. It is human dignity that allows a Christian to disagree with another person while still respecting their humanity.

Here are some basic biblical, theological, and philosophical truths that every parent should know:

- Human dignity is a creational property woven into the fabric of biblical creation order.

- Dignity is a property that exists *only* because God declares human beings to be made in his image.
- Dignity is not a property determined by any attribute apart from existence itself.
- Apart from the Christian worldview, upholding the dignity of the human person is a mere invention of human thought without any firm grounding or absolute foundation.
- "Dignity" for the secular individual requires *faith* in something that a secular individual cannot adequately account for apart from the arbitrary assertion that dignity exists.

MEMORY VERSE

So God created man in his own image,
  in the image of God he created him;
  male and female he created them. (Gen. 1:27)

THE FIRST FLOOR
Biblical Truths

- God created all humans in his image. Humans can think and love one another (Gen. 1:26–28).
- God created all humans worthy of respect. Respect means to be kind and polite.
- Humans deserve respect because God created us in his image.

- We should be kind, polite, and loving to everyone *simply* because God created them.
- Every human matters to God (John 3:16).

Conversation Starters

- How did God create all humans? What can humans do since we are created in God's image? What are some ways that we can love one another?
- What does respect mean? How can you be kind and polite to others?
- Why do humans deserve respect and love? Did you do anything to deserve respect and love?
- Why should we be kind, polite, and loving to everyone? How can you be kind, polite, and loving to others?
- Who matters to God? Why does every single human matter to God?

THE SECOND FLOOR

Biblical Truths

- God created all humans in his image. Human beings are created with the capacity to reason with their minds and love one another relationally (Gen. 1:26–28).
- God created all humans worthy of dignity. Human dignity means that everyone is worthy of honor and respect.
- Humans have dignity *simply* because God created them in his image. This truth is unbreakable and unchangeable because it is a divine truth from God.

- Every human matters in God's eyes. We should not look down on someone because he or she looks different, thinks differently, acts differently, or does anything else differently than you or I do. Others deserve honor and respect simply because God created them (James 2:1–13).
- As Christians, we are called to speak truth and seek peace with others, even if we disagree (Rom. 12:18; 1 Cor. 13:6).

Conversation Starters

- How did God create humans? What does it mean to be created in God's image? How are humans different from all other created beings? What does it mean to reason with our minds? What does it mean to love one another relationally?
- God created humans worthy of what? What does human dignity mean? What is honor and respect? How can you show someone honor and respect?
- How do humans have dignity? Where does this human dignity come from? How can we be sure that this is an unbreakable and unchangeable truth?
- Why does every human matter to God? Why should we not look down on others who are different from us? Have you ever encountered someone who is different from you? How was he or she different? Did you think you were better in some way? Do you now see how he or she deserved honor and respect just like you?
- What does it mean to speak truth and seek peace? Do you think you will ever disagree with someone while talking about the Bible? Have you ever disagreed with someone?

How did you handle that? Read Col. 4:5–6 and make a plan about how to have a conversation with someone who might not believe the way you believe.

THE THIRD FLOOR

Biblical Truths

- *Imago Dei* means that humans are created in the image and likeness of God. Humans are created to reflect God morally, spiritually, and intellectually. Humans are rational and relational beings, we have a purpose, and we can partake in fellowship with God. *Imago Dei* is the Latin translation for "image of God" (Gen. 1:26–28).

- Human dignity is showing honor and respect to everyone simply because they have been made in God's image. There is nothing anyone can do to earn dignity or lose dignity. Everyone has dignity because of *imago Dei*.

- Human dignity is woven into the fabric of the creational order. God confers dignity at the moment of creation. Dignity exists because God declares it, and it does not exist apart from God.

- All human beings deserve dignity. We should never look down on someone because of skin color, physical differences, cognitive differences, or anything else that the world may deem "less than." People are worthy because God called them worthy the very moment they were created. All human beings matter and have value because of *imago Dei* (James 2:1–13).

- Human dignity is the foundation of Christians standing against social evils or assault on image bearers. Human dignity was introduced through Jewish and Christian teaching and revolutionized the world with the idea of human "rights": equal protection under the rule of law that allows human beings to flourish.
- It is the doctrine of human dignity that led Christians to form schools and universities, charities devoted to repairing social breakdown, and hospitals for healing people.
- As Christians, God calls us to a high standard of conversation with others. We are to show others dignity even when we disagree with them: "Walk in wisdom toward outsiders, making the best use of the time. Let your speech always be gracious, seasoned with salt, so that you may know how you ought to answer each person" (Col. 4:5–6).

Conversation Starters

- What does *imago Dei* mean? What are the unique characteristics of humans? What does it look like to be made with a purpose and partake in fellowship with God? What is the English translation of *imago Dei*?
- What does human dignity mean? How does someone receive human dignity? Who decides who deserves dignity? What can you do to earn or lose dignity? How can you show dignity to others?
- How is human dignity woven into the fabric of the creational order? How does God confer dignity at creation? Explain how dignity exists because of God and not apart from him.

- Who deserves dignity? Have you ever seen someone who is different from you? How was that person different? Do you think that person deserves dignity? Why or why not? Have you ever witnessed a situation where someone did not receive or show dignity? What did you do? Have you ever treated someone unfairly? Explain how *imago Dei* gives humans value.
- How did Christianity and human dignity revolutionize the world with the idea of human rights?
- Describe the higher standard of conversation that God requires of Christians. Have you ever experienced a disagreeable conversation? How did you handle that? Discuss Colossians 4:5–6. How can these verses help you with conversations in the future?

RECOMMENDED RESOURCES

Darling, Daniel. *The Dignity Revolution: Reclaiming God's Rich Vision for Humanity*. London: The Good Book Company, 2018.

Hoekema, Anthony. *Created in God's Image*. Grand Rapids, MI: Eerdmans, 1994.

Kaczor, Christopher. *A Defense of Dignity: Creating Life, Destroying Life, and Protecting the Rights of Conscience*. Notre Dame, IN: University of Notre Dame Press, 2013.

Kilner, John. *Dignity and Destiny: Humanity in the Image of God*. Grand Rapids, MI: Eerdmans, 2015.

Snead, Carter O. *What It Means to Be Human: The Case for the Body in Public Bioethics*. Harvard University Press, 2020.

2

Abortion

IT ALL BEGAN WITH something as simple as yard signs.

Recently, the state of Kentucky, where our family lives, had a major election where voters had to decide whether our state constitution would recognize abortion as a right. Things got really intense, as you might imagine. Our neighborhood reflected the polarized climate of the state: some homes had pro-life signs while others had pro-choice signs.

Our eight-year-old, Catherine, asked the question: "Dad, why do a lot of homes have signs in their yard?"

We were one of those yards that had a pro-life sign.

My eyes locked with Christian's as we sat on the back patio, we took a deep breath, and I began. "Catherine, this may be hard for you to understand, but there are some people who think that a baby in a mommy's tummy can be killed."

Catherine looked (rightly) puzzled. She replied, "Why would any mommy or any daddy want to do that? Don't they love their baby?"

Christian responded, "Well, sweet girl, there are some people who think that having a baby could be really hard on their lives; that they may not be ready to be a mom or dad, or they may not have enough money to be a mommy or daddy."

Catherine still looked confused. She couldn't get it through her little mind that a mom and dad would not want their baby. She intuitively recognized that if there's a baby, then that life is precious and should be valued. We proceeded to tell Catherine at that point that her mom and dad do not agree with people who support this attitude toward children. We told her that even though there are people who think that way, we have to do our best to change their minds respectfully, peacefully, and firmly while still loving them even if we really disagree with them. She seemed to understand that. What we stressed to her is that this issue is not something that should ever cause her to wonder whether her mom and dad had ever considered whether her life was worthwhile. We stressed our total love, joy, and delight in her.

As expected, our little social butterfly moved on to the next thing.

BIBLICAL TEACHING OVERVIEW

One of the most stand-out truths of all of Scripture is that God is the author and giver of life (Acts 3:15). Christians anchor their belief in the value of created life in the same way that we honor God as the Creator of everything that has ever existed. To value life is to honor and respect God's sovereignty over what he has created.

The sanctity of human life begins with God the Creator. The most foundational scriptural truth Christians should know is that Scrip-

26

ture teaches that all humans are made in God's image (Gen. 1:26–28). This is where everything hinges on the Christian's belief about abortion. Being made in God's image is what separates humanity from the rest of creation. The sun, the earth, and the birds are not made in God's image; only humans are. Monkeys do not contemplate the meaning of life's purpose. Human beings possess a distinct value in the sheer fact of our existence that makes us important. Scripture teaches the marvelous truth that humans possess value, dignity, and worth not because of anything we do to earn it, but because God is the type of God who simply loves what he created. People do not possess more dignity if they have greater intelligence or are better looking than someone else. No, according to Scripture, a radical equality exists that every human being shares by virtue of being created. The disabled teen and the Olympic athlete are equal in God's eyes. Christianity does not separate dignity or personhood between the unborn and the born—that's a division that Scripture does not recognize. In fact, the Bible teaches that the child in the womb was created by God and considered a member of the human species (Ps. 139; Luke 1:41–44).

Scripture always prohibits the unlawful taking of human life. What makes abortion so grievously wicked is that it not only defaces the image of God in persons; it robs those image-bearers of the life they are owed for themselves and the life given to them by God. The reason Scripture condemns murder is that it robs God of his authority over life and denies what is owed to human beings: the right to live. Without enshrining this most fundamental prin-ciple—the right *not* to be wantonly killed but rather to experience life—the whole purpose of safeguarding our existence is called into question. Existence is something that living persons, under normal conditions, desire to continue. In numerous places, Scripture unequivocally condemns and prohibits the unlawful taking of human life (Gen. 9:5–6; Ex. 20:13). Murder is an injustice, and since abortion is the unlawful taking of innocent human life, it too is an unjust action.

There is a precious line that must be drawn: either human life is intrinsically valuable for its own sake and, therefore, worthy of protection. Or else human life's value is expendable or discardable by some other set of conditions determined by human authority. But left to the decision of human authority, there is no assurance that political regimes will maintain the commitment to respecting unborn life. One cannot permit abortion without inviting the possibility of taking innocent life elsewhere. Indeed, the logic of abortion is so flimsy and outrageous that if one were asked whether it would be okay to kill a toddler (something we think most everyone would answer with a strong, *no!*), the types of arguments for killing an unborn child also apply to the logic of killing a toddler. For example, if a child is not protected by laws against homicide until after birth, what is it about being born that magically confers legal protection? After all, the child *outside* of the womb is the same child that was *inside* the womb.

At its most basic (and yet, very logically sound) argument, the case against abortion goes like this:

1. An unborn child is a member of the human species.
2. It is morally wrong to take the life of an innocent member of the human species.

3. Abortion takes the life of a member of the human species.
4. Therefore, abortion is immoral.[1]

Christians are called to defend the weak. Proverbs 24:11 teaches that Christians are to

rescue those who are being taken away to death;
hold back those who are stumbling to the slaughter.

We are called to protect the vulnerable. We do so out of a belief that human life is something to be cherished, not discarded at will. The Christian church is at its best when we speak up for the voiceless, the oppressed, and the marginalized. One of the most consistent teachings throughout the history of the Christian church is the value of human life. From the Bible to the earliest beginnings of the church, one of the most distinguishing characteristics of Christianity was its concern for human dignity—the unborn, children, the protection of women, and care for the poor.

————

Here are some basic biblical, theological, and philosophical truths every parent should know:

• It is a scientific fact that life begins at conception.
• Every human being, whether born or unborn, possesses equal dignity.

1   This argument is adapted from a similar argument that my friend Francis J. Beckwith makes in *Defending Life: A Moral and Legal Case against Abortion Choice* (New York: Cambridge University Press, 200), xii.

- An unborn child shares the same essential nature as any other human being.
- An unborn human is not a "potential" human but a full human at a lesser stage of development.
- It is a violation of justice to inflict lethal violence upon a child.
- Scripture prohibits the unlawful taking of innocent life, which necessarily includes abortion.
- Christians are called to defend the unborn against cultural forces that would destroy them.
- Whatever difficult circumstances exist does not justify taking the life of an unborn child.
- Christians are called to care for women and men who find themselves considering an abortion.
- There is no justification for taking an unborn child's life, regardless of the circumstances that led to the child's conception. A mother or father's situation is not made better by murdering someone else.

MEMORY VERSE

Rescue those who are being taken away to death;
   hold back those who are stumbling to the slaughter.
      (Prov. 24:11)

THE FIRST FLOOR
Biblical Truths

- All people are created by God (Acts 3:15).

- All people are created in the image of God (Gen. 1:26–28).
- All babies are people created in the image of God, even in their mommy's belly (Ps. 139:13–16).
- If we believe in God, then we believe in taking care of the babies and people that God created (Prov. 24:11).

Conversation Starters

- Who created us?
- Who else did God create?
- Is a baby in a mommy's belly a real person?
- What can we do to care for others?

THE SECOND FLOOR

Biblical Truths

- All people are created in the image of God (Gen. 1:26–28).
- All babies are people created in the image of God, even in their mother's womb (Ps. 139:13–16).
- Every person possesses equal dignity (worth, honor, and respect).
- It is not okay to kill other people that God created (Ex. 20:13).
- If we believe in God, then we believe in taking care of the babies and people that God created (Prov. 24:11).

Conversation Starters

- Who did God create?
- What does it mean to be "created in the image of God"?

- When do babies become real people?
- Who has the authority to give and take life?
- What can we do to care for others?

THE THIRD FLOOR

Biblical Truths

- All people are created in the image of God and possess equal dignity (worth, honor, and respect) (Gen. 1:26–28).
- Babies are human at the point of conception and created in the image of God.
- An unborn child is no less human than a child that is born; an unborn child is a human being at a lesser stage of development.
- A child in a woman's body has a right to life (Isa. 44:2).
- Scripture says that murder is a sin against God and others at all ages of life (Gen. 9:5–6).
- Abortion is the murder of the unborn baby in the mother's womb.
- Humans do not have an absolute right to do whatever they want with their bodies—especially when a third party is concerned, like a child (1 Cor. 6:12–20).
- Government has a responsibility to protect human life by passing laws that protect all persons equally, including the unborn child (Rom. 13:1–7).
- If we believe in God and call ourselves Christians, then we believe in defending the unborn.

- Christians should provide material assistance to mothers and fathers considering an abortion, whether by direct assistance or by helping contribute to Christian mercy ministries that help people in times of need (James 2:14–17).

Conversation Starters

- What does it mean to be "created in the image of God" and possess dignity?
- How would you describe "life at conception" to a friend who doesn't believe babies have a right to life until they are born?
- Why don't the circumstances of a child's conception change the child's right to life?
- What does Scripture say about murder, abortion, and the consequences of both?
- What is the purpose of the government?
- What can we do to care for women and men considering abortion, women and men post-abortion, and women, men, and their babies who decided to choose life against the odds?

RECOMMENDED RESOURCES

Alcorn, Randy. *Prolife Answers to Prochoice Arguments*. Colorado Springs: Multnomah, 2000.

Anderson, Ryan T., and Alexandria DeSanctis, *Tearing Us Apart: How Abortion Harms Everything and Solves Nothing*. Washington, DC: Regnery Publishing, 2023.

Beckwith, Francis. *Defending Life: A Moral and Legal Case against Abortion Choice*. New York: Cambridge University Press, 2007.

George, Robert P., and Christopher Tollefsen. *Embryo: A Defense of Human Life*. Princeton, NJ: Witherspoon Institute, 2011.

Klusendorf, Scott. *The Case for Life: Equipping Christians to Engage the Culture*. Wheaton, IL: Crossway, 2023.

Schaeffer, Francis, and C. Everett Koop. *Whatever Happened to the Human Race?* Wheaton, IL: Crossway, 2021.

Sproul, R. C. *Abortion: A Rational Look at an Emotional Issue*. Sanford, FL: Ligonier Ministries, 2022.

3

Sexuality

NO BIGGER LIE has been told in our culture than the lie that sexual freedom is the source of personal happiness and fulfillment.

Nothing could be further from the truth.

Just look around you. Sexual confusion has resulted in a perfect storm producing unending moral relativism and personal regret while soaring social and economic inequality sorts people into groups determined predominantly by whether persons were raised in a married household. The individual and cultural ramifications of sexuality require us to speak the truth and confront error.

Neither of us has heard from friends whose years of sexual promiscuity are looked back on with anything other than regret. What is interesting to observe is the growing chorus of voices, even non-Christian voices, in our society that are beginning to question whether the so-called ecstasy of sexual freedom has overpromised and under-delivered.

Because of how unabashedly and unashamedly our culture is awash in sexual confusion, it's important to consider how much earlier it will be necessary to talk with your children about sexuality. As I (Andrew) will often tell parents, "You can catechize your children about God's standards for sexuality, or the world will catechize your children with its standards for sexuality." Regardless of the source, eventually, kids figure it out. Better they hear from you than from someone else.

The good news is this: cultural controversy doesn't mean theological complexity. The Bible's teaching about sexuality is quite clear. It is not that it is hard to discern but that in a fallen age, it is hard to obey. The forces bearing down on parents to lead their families make this subject increasingly difficult to navigate. When you factor in the personal battles that every person must wage to pursue sexual holiness, secular critics that depict Christianity as hateful, and progressive Christian voices who misinterpret Scripture to make it align with the spirit of the age, we know parents have their work cut out for them.

BIBLICAL TEACHING OVERVIEW

Sexuality is a gift from God. Our sexual design is nothing to be ashamed of. Because it is a gift to be received instead of a blank canvas to be experimented with, it is to be stewarded according to God's will. Christians believe the Bible's teaching governing sexuality offers the only pathway for true human flourishing. When society rejects or casts off what Scripture teaches regarding sexuality, society is not simply disagreeing with Christians but rejecting the limits and boundaries God set for all of creation (Rom. 1:18–32). We cannot be happy living against the Creator's will. We might think we can, but the deceitfulness of sin is that it leads us down a path on which we do not see or feel the immediate consequences of until afterward (Heb. 3:13). We see this groaning of creation all around us when the sexual misuse of our bodies becomes normal and routine: women are treated as objects by men acting as sexual conquerors instead of protectors, serial fornication cheapens what is meant to be a profound union, marriages fail to form altogether, and children go motherless or fatherless or are even aborted.

God created human beings to be sexual, therefore, sexuality is good under God's design. In the opening two chapters of Genesis, sexuality and marriage come immediately into view (Gen. 1:26–28; 2:18–24). There isn't one without the other. In other words, the fact that God made us male and female and with the desire to sexually unite is not an afterthought. The complementary design of male and female is what makes reproduction possible. Both need the other in order to "fit" together sexually in what Scripture refers to as the husband and wife becoming "one flesh" (Gen. 2:24). Since God is the author of our sexuality, there is no shame in recognizing the fact of our sexual desires. Scripture, rather, understands that the direction in which those sexual desires are channeled is to be chosen with a view toward God's will, not simply whatever humanity wills for itself or whatever desires come "naturally." All of this suggests that rightly ordering one's sexuality is to recognize God's rightful authority over creation and our bodies (1 Cor. 6:12–20).

God's pattern for sexuality upholds the marriage of husband and wife as the exclusive grounds for sexual activity. It's not *only* that God created human beings to be sexual; it's that God defines the exclusive context for sexual activity within the covenantal marriage union of husband and wife. The fact that marriage is what secures the context for our sexuality speaks to what marriage *is*: the union of one man and one woman who become husband and wife and father and mother to the children their union produces. According to Scripture, the marriage union is intended to be complementary, sexually exclusive between the spouses only, and permanent. "One flesh" that Genesis 2:24 speaks of the husband and wife becoming is not just a powerful metaphor. It's speaking about the comprehensive nature of what marriage is: an embodied union of two persons who become one, literally. A husband and wife's bodies united together in an intimate act is what makes them "one." While pleasure is one purpose of sexuality, it is not the only or even the highest purpose of sexuality—reproduction is. That profound oneness is what consummates their marriage, what ratifies their marriage covenant each time they unite sexually, and what makes reproduction possible. Scripture treats all of these aspects as simultaneous realities. In the New Testament, we gain a new understanding of marriage's significance in God's eyes. It's not just a creational reality; it reflects a redemptive reality as well. According to the apostle Paul, earthly marriages mirror the divine marriage of the Christ-church union (Eph. 5:22–33).

God's pattern for sexuality is freeing and tied to human flourishing. Because of where sexuality and marriage enter the picture in the Bible, its place is saying something very significant: Sexuality and marriage are guided by a creational ethic that governs the entire Bible's teaching on sexuality. Once we understand the nature of God's blueprint for marriage, it makes sense why deviations from God's creational order are considered sinful—they go against God's original, intended plan. But we don't focus on what's gone wrong. We should begin with what is the Bible's picture of rightly-ordered sexuality. The Bible does not target any particular class of sexual sinners; it views all of humanity as sexually broken. When human beings pursue sexuality as God intends, they are safeguarding themselves from the tragedies that come from misusing, misdirecting, or abusing one's sexuality. Understood on a social scale, when culture rejects God's pattern for sexual holiness devastation results.

Christians believe God's plan for sexuality is not arbitrary or restrictive. Rather, following God's pattern is the most freeing way to live. God's plan allows us to encounter the blessings of marriage and family life. Sin distorts our desires, but exercising faith means trusting God's plan. Biblical sexuality is the only pathway that leads to true personal and cultural flourishing.

Rightly-ordered sexuality brings God glory. God calls us to live completely for him in glad submission. As the Bible teaches, we Christians are not our own; we were bought with a price (1 Cor. 6:18–20). The call of the Christian, then, is to glorify God with the use of our bodies (1 Cor. 6:19–20). Rather than our sexuality serving ourselves selfishly, our sexuality is meant to serve God's purposes in treating our sexuality as a gift reserved only for our spouse. Every sexual desire and act must be done with a view of pursuing God's honor and glory in accordance with his standards. We are to embrace God's pattern with joy. How we use our bodies is a measure of our submission to the Lord and our understanding the true purpose for our design—which is to build families and healthy cultures, experience the joys of our embodiment, and ultimately glorify him. At the end of this, sexuality is a gift from the Lord: children, unity, pleasure, companionship, delight—the well-ordered family are kindnesses from him.

The gospel affirms the creational order for sexuality and marriage and offers a pathway for us to live lives of sexual holiness. Jesus affirms the creational structure of God's plan for sexuality in Matthew 19:4–6. The apostle Paul argues that it is the indwelling of the Holy Spirit that allows us to live lives of sexual holiness (1 Cor. 6:12–20; Titus 2:11–14). Because our bodies are bought with a price as Christians, we are to honor the Lord with them, and we have the power of the Holy Spirit within us, enabling us to do so.

———

Here are some basic biblical, theological, and philosophical truths every parent should know:

- Christian sexual ethics offer a positive framework for channeling one's sexual design.
- Christian sexual ethics are not about legalistic no's; but about safeguarding a gift that God has given in the design and purpose of the body.
- Marriage is the complementary, permanent, and monogamous union of husband and wife.
- It is the complementary design of the body that makes a husband and wife sexually fit for each other.

- There is a fixed and authoritative moral logic to the Bible's blueprint for sexuality that connects our design to our desire for procreation and companionship.
- The pattern for sexual obedience is marital by design in Scripture. Biblical sexual desire is for one's spouse, not simply a generic opposite-sex desire.
- While sexuality and marriage are gifts from God, Scripture does not depict either as the comprehensive basis for one's identity or human fulfillment. Sexual purity, celibacy, and chastity within marriage are all equal pathways to human flourishing.
- Marriage does not have an elastic or evolving definition. Marriage just *is* by the design of God, and apart from this definition, marriage unravels into simply whatever emotional union exists between any number of persons.
- Defining sexual morality apart from marriage being the biblical grounds for sexual activity leads to radical moral relativism, as we see in today's culture, where virtually all sexuality is normalized.
- Pursuing and exercising sexual self-control is the Bible's ethic for one's sexual design, not merely self-autonomy and consent.

NOTE: Parents, this is a good time to discuss abstinence being the only way to effectively remain pure. But we have a bubble to burst: if you think that the ultimate goal of parenting when it comes to navigating the topic of sexuality is only to keep your children from intercourse, and that's all there is to "purity," you are woefully short of the goal line. Sexual sin includes all the other things that lead up to intercourse, things that happen with eyes, hands, mouths, and genitals. You need to be talking with your kids about sexual purity in a way that includes abstinence from all sexual activity, not just intercourse itself. Your kids may not be partaking in the sexual activities that lead to sex, but they probably know about it. They do not live in a protective chamber. Talk to them specifically about those things, no matter how uncomfortable the conversation is for you or them. They need to hear from you, or they will hear from the world.

MEMORY VERSE

Or do you not know that your body is a temple of the Holy Spirit within you, whom you have from God? You are not your own, for you were bought with a price. So glorify God in your body. (1 Cor. 6:19–20)

THE FIRST FLOOR

Biblical Truths

- God is the Creator (Gen. 1:1).
- God created our bodies, and they are good (Gen. 1:26–28).
- God created boys and girls differently, and that is good (Gen. 2:18–24) .
- God created daddies and mommies to get married, have children, and take care of their families (Gen. 1:28; Ex. 20:12, 14).
- God wants our families to bring him glory.

Conversation Starters

- Who is the Creator? What are some things God created?
- Who did God create? What parts of your body did God create? Is your body good?
- How are boys and girls different? Does God want us to be different?
- What does God want daddies and mommies to do? What are some ways your daddy and mommy take care of your family?
- How can our family bring God glory?

THE SECOND FLOOR

Biblical Truths

- God created our bodies male and female with different physical parts to fit together, and it is good within God's plan for marriage (Gen. 2:18–24).
- God created us with desires and attractions for the opposite sex, and it is good within God's plan for marriage (Gen. 1:26–28).
- God created males and females to become one flesh in marriage, have children, and care for their families. Our families should bring him honor and glory (Gen. 1:28; Ex. 20:12, 14).
- Our bodies should be saved for God's original, natural, and good plan for marriage.
- We must use our bodies to bring glory and honor to God because we were bought with a price when Jesus died for us on the cross (1 Cor. 6:12–20).

Conversation Starters

- How did God create males and females the same and different? What is physically different? How do males and females fit together? How is that good in God's plan for marriage?
- Is it okay to have feelings and attractions for the opposite sex? What makes those desires and attractions good? Have you ever liked or been attracted to anyone?
- What is God's ultimate plan for marriage? What does it mean to be one flesh? How do parents care for their families? How do we as your parents care for you? How can your family bring God honor and glory?
- Why does God want us to save our bodies for marriage? How can we do that?
- How were our bodies bought with a price? How can our bodies bring honor and glory to God?

THE THIRD FLOOR

Biblical Truths

- God created the male and female to be complementary. The two bodies sexually fit together in the union of one flesh in the good plan of marriage (Gen. 2:18–24).
- God created males and females with attractions and sexual desires for one another which are good within God's design for marriage. Sexuality is a good gift from God for the purpose of marriage between one man and one woman. Marriage is meant to be a one-flesh union

44

that is complementary, permanent, and monogamous (Gen. 1:26–28).

- God created males and females to enter into a one-flesh union in marriage, bear any children God may provide, and bring him glory and honor as they care for their families.

- Sexual attractions, desires, and activity are good and right within the confines of a one-flesh union between a husband and wife. Rightly-ordered sexuality shows our submission to Christ's authority over creation and our bodies (1 Cor. 6:12–20).

- We should safeguard our bodies for the gift of God's original, natural, and good plan of marriage. This is rightly-ordered sexuality that allows us to enjoy the blessings of marriage and family life (Heb. 13:4).

- We must use self-control to safeguard our bodies and pursue holiness and purity as God intends. Your body does not belong to you, we each have been bought with a price, and we belong to God. The Holy Spirit gives us the power to keep our bodies pure until we enter into a one-flesh union so we can enjoy the blessings of marriage and family life (1 Thess. 4:3–5).

- Sin distorts our sexual desires and can lead us to misuse, misdirect, and/or abuse our sexuality. All humanity is sexually broken and in need of redemption. (Eph. 5:3–6).

- The Christian sexual ethic is the only way for personal human and cultural flourishing. When any and all sexuality outside of God's natural plan of creation becomes normalized, it leads to a breakdown of marriage, family, and culture (Rom. 1:18–32).

- Ultimately, purity of the heart is what believers should be striving for. When we submit to God's authority and let Jesus completely transform our hearts, purity and holiness will flow out of our transformed hearts and seep into all areas of our lives. Sexual purity is an overflow, a byproduct, and a good consequence of the transformed heart (2 Cor. 7:1).

Conversation Starters

- How are males and females complementary? How do they sexually fit together? Why is this good in marriage? What does "one flesh" mean? How could this be a bad thing outside of marriage?
- How is sexuality a good gift from God? Why is sexuality for the purpose of marriage between one man and one woman? What happens when sexuality is taken out of marriage between one man and one woman? What is marriage? What does *complementary, permanent,* and *monogamous* mean? What happens when one or two of those three things is not present in marriage?
- What is the ultimate purpose of the marriage union? How do parents care for their families? How do we as your parents care for our family? How can our family bring God glory and honor?
- Why is it that sexual attractions, desires, and activity are *only* good within marriage? What does a "one-flesh union" mean? Why does a one-flesh union only work with a husband and wife, not a husband and husband or wife and wife? Who created you and your body? How does this rightly-ordered sexuality show your submission to God's authority?

- What does it mean to safeguard your body? How can you do that? What kind of holiness and purity does God want from you? How is saving your body sexually for your marriage holy and pure? What does it mean that your body does not belong to you and has been bought with a price? What are the blessings of marriage and family life that God has in store for you? How can the Holy Spirit help you maintain purity until marriage so you can receive those blessings?
- How can sin distort our sexual desires? What examples have you seen where sin has led to misuse, misdirection, or even the abuse of sexuality? If all humanity is broken and in need of redemption, how and where will they find that? How can you tell others about that redemption? Have you ever experienced sexual sin? How can we (your parents) help you?
- Why is the Christian sexual ethic the only way for personal and cultural flourishing? Why does everything fall apart when we stray from God's natural plan of creation?
- Are you striving after a pure heart and a pure life? Have you submitted to God's authority, and are you allowing Jesus to transform your heart? Are purity and holiness seeping into all the areas of your life? Is sexual purity a byproduct of your pure heart?

RECOMMENDED RESOURCES

Anderson, Ryan T., Sherif Girgis, and Robert P. George, *What Is Marriage? Man and Woman: A Defense*. New York: Encounter, 2012.

Ash, Christopher. *Marriage: Sex in the Service of God.* Vancouver, Canada: Regent College Publishing, 2005.

Budziszewski, J. *On the Meaning of Sex.* Washington, DC: Regnery Gateway, 2014.

Burk, Denny. *What Is the Meaning of Sex?* Wheaton, IL: Crossway, 2013.

Köstenberger, Andreas, and David W. Jones, *God, Marriage, and Family: Rebuilding the Biblical Foundation.* Wheaton, IL: Crossway, 2010.

Walker, Andrew T. "Gender and Sexuality," The Gospel Coalition. https://www.thegospelcoalition.org.

Wilson, Todd. *Mere Sexuality: Rediscovering the Christian Vision of Sexuality.* Grand Rapids, MI: Zondervan, 2017.

Yuan, Christopher. *Holy Sexuality and the Gospel: Sex, Desire, and Relationships Shaped by God's Grand Story.* New York: Multnomah, 2018.

4

Gender

WE HAVE A very close family friend named Allie.[1]

Allie does not "fit the profile" of every feminine stereotype. She's physically tougher than most women we know (and perhaps, a lot of men). She has tattoos. She has a physically demanding job where she builds furniture. She's just as comfortable in shorts and a T-shirt as she is in a dress. She knows she projects a "masculine vibe" by our culture's standards.

At the same time, Allie is a Christian and knows she's a woman. In no sense is she trying to communicate ambiguity in how she presents herself. Furthermore, she also enjoys activities that are associated with femininity. When she dresses nicely for a wedding or night out with friends, she looks very feminine. She can rock a pair of high heels better than any other woman we know.

The world doesn't know what to do with Allie because she does not fit into all the neat little boxes that culture puts "gender" into.

---

1 The name of Allie has been changed to protect her privacy, though we have permission to share this story.

But just because Allie doesn't conform to every gender stereotype does not make her any less of a woman. Similarly, I (Andrew) don't enjoy a lot of activities associated with typical masculinity in our culture. I am not a big sports fan. I don't like to hunt. You could not pay me to do jujitsu, despite many friends in my church inviting me. I love to sing. I like musicals. But I do like JEEP Wranglers. Are sports and vehicles the essence of what it means to be a man? What if a woman really likes football (like our friend Paige)?

Our culture gets gender both right and wrong. Our culture is correct to observe that there are general actions, tendencies, and appearances for males and females, but a failure to conform to every action and every appearance associated with a gender stereotype does not mean that one is evading gender altogether. The solution is neither rigid stereotyping, gender fluidity, nor the total suppression of gender.

No word has greater confusion around it than the word "gender" does in our culture. "Gender reveal parties," "same-gender marriage," "gender is socially constructed," or "gender exists on a spectrum" are all examples of how "gender" gets used in our culture, and these are only a few of the ways. Given its usage, "gender" can mean anything anyone wants it to mean. It's a term that individuals pour into what they want.

While chapter 7 will focus on gender in the context of the transgender revolution, the purpose of this chapter is to set forth a positive biblical vision for gender because of how convoluted the term is.

BIBLICAL TEACHING OVERVIEW

When God acts to create humankind in Genesis, Scripture declares that humanity is made in two differentiated forms: male and female. This distinction is the primary classification for differentiating humanity. Man and woman in Genesis are identifiable and unchanging categories defined by their unique bodily characteristics. These characteristics are the result of genetic realities present from the earliest moments in the mother's womb. Sex chromosomes encode a binary that directs either male or female development. The first chapter of the Bible reflects the same realities revealed in genetics and biology—that human beings come in two genres, male or female.

As Genesis 1:26–28 states:

Then God said, "Let us make man in our image, after our likeness. And let them have dominion over the fish of the sea and over the birds of the heavens and over the livestock and over all the earth and over every creeping thing that creeps on the earth."

So God created man in his own image,
in the image of God he created him;
male and female he created them.

And God blessed them. And God said to them, "Be fruitful and multiply and fill the earth and subdue it, and have dominion over the fish of the sea and over the birds of the heavens and over every living thing that moves on the earth."

It should not be glossed over that the identification of man and woman is tied to the calling that their bodies are suited to fulfill. Their embodied form is what makes the call to fruitful multiplication and dominion possible. Man and woman join together in marriage to become husband and wife to produce children and, likewise, future families that fill the earth and rule over it on behalf of God. Reproductive organization is central to male and female identity. This is not only a biblical truth within the text of Scripture but also a biological truth observable within creation.

Male and female embodiment is a gift from God. To be male or female reflects the givenness of a fixed creational order that we are to embrace as a gracious gift of God to creation. There is no generic unsexed body. Neither does Scripture give us license to see humanity transcending (or bypassing) the reality that comes from our embodiment. All bodies are either male or female. Gender reflects the orderliness of creation. As Abigail Favale says about creation order in Genesis,

> This order is good, intentionally and patiently called into being by an uncreated Creator. Human beings, male and female, are endowed with a unique dignity, marked by the image of their Creator, and entrusted with the sacred work of cultivating life. Sexual difference is not an extraneous or faulty feature of the cosmos but an essential part of its goodness.[2]

The body reveals identity, purpose, and calling. As Genesis 1–2 depicts, maleness and femaleness are not psychological or emotional states of mind but embodied realities and signposts to what our bodies are for: earthly dominion through reproduction and family formation. While males and females are equal in worth and

2   Abigail Favale, *The Genesis of Gender: A Christian Theory* (San Francisco: Ignatius Press, 2022), 36.

dignity, their bodily design indicates that their capacities are not all the same. While men can nurture, women just are, by nature, better nurturers because God's design for motherhood is tied to femaleness. While women can protect others, men just are, by nature and capacity, better suited for protection. This is why men's athletic records always surpass women's athletic achievements. This difference is not a statement of moral worth about the sexes; it is a statement of fact proceeding from our different bodies. Societies come to naturally accommodate the social realities that stem from our embodiment. Misogyny, feminism, and androgyny are against God's created order.[3] Assigning moral superiority based on some aspect of our sex (e.g., misogyny, feminism) is not allowed by Scripture nor is suppressing the difference of our sexes (e.g., androgyny). All in all, God's design of males and females results in there being unique aptitudes tied to bodily sex. It is these unique and complementary aptitudes that create unique responsibilities and moral obligations that are tied to our embodiment.

"Gender" is first and foremost determined by biological sex. Gender is merely the cultural manifestation tied to biological sex that every culture inevitably manifests. But we do not define a male and female preeminently by their activities or expression but by their embodiment. Males, to be sure, will tend toward acting masculinely but masculine actions are first tied to the body's natural giftings and aptitudes—not chiefly a set of cultural characteristics that can change from one culture to the next. This is why it's popular for men to wear kilts in Scotland, but in an American

3   By "mysogyny," we are referring to any worldview—Christian or otherwise—that denigrates the unique giftings of women and their calling to be vice-regents alongside men.

context, kilts would be associated with feminine attire. It isn't that a piece of clothing is inherently feminine or masculine; it's that kilts or skirts take on masculine or feminine properties by virtue of the culture.

Biblical gender expression has broader contours than modern culture's tendency toward gender stereotyping. Take King David as an example. David is simultaneously a ruthless warrior, a poet, and a musician. We should understand that not all males will live up to male stereotypes, and the same is true for females. Not all men like to hunt, and not all women like to cook. Gender norms can manifest differently from one culture to another. What every culture attempts to do, however, is culturally express the reality of maleness and femaleness. The Bible calls us to obey gender norms insofar as gender norms are not aiding or abetting gender confusion (Deut. 22:5; 1 Cor. 11:3–16). Gender norms are important to maintain because they reflect the natural tendency for cultures to acknowledge the innate differences between males and females.

The logic of bodily sex difference helps explain the moral logic of biblical sexual ethics overall. The normative expression for sexual relations in Scripture is tied to the design of the body. Male and female bodies are designed for one another in a reciprocal, complementary, and life-giving way. We understand what biblical sexuality is by respecting the natural design of the body. The end for which the body is organized—namely, reproduction—tells us what sexual actions are, therefore, proper to the body and which actions are immoral.

Jesus affirms the Genesis pattern for sexual embodiment. In Matthew 19:4–6, Jesus affirms and upholds as normative the reality that male and female are creational categories rooted in the design of the body.

> He answered, "Have you not read that he who created them from the beginning made them male and female, and said, 'Therefore a man shall leave his father and his mother and hold fast to his wife, and the two shall become one flesh'? So they are no longer two but one flesh. What therefore God has joined together, let not man separate." (Matt. 19:4–6)

Here are some basic biblical, theological, and philosophical truths every parent should know:

- The Bible's portrayal of gender expression is rooted in one's biological sex.
- Gender is predominantly an embodied reality before it is a cultural reality.
- Human bodies are organized according to their reproductive potential.
- Equality of the sexes does not mean sameness as to roles or abilities.
- Male and female are not cultural constructs but are embedded realities knit into the creation order.
- Defining male and female identity apart from biology leads to an inability to concretely identify male and female.

- Male and female embodiment influences social roles and behaviors.
- It is wrong for men and women to view gender expression as totally arbitrary since Scripture does positively teach Christians to abide by gender norms that are determined by cultural context.
- The design of the body is like a moral map that tells us how to use our bodies properly.
- It is okay if every male does not live up to every male stereotype. The same is true of females.

MEMORY VERSE

He answered, "Have you not read that he who created them from the beginning made them male and female, and said, 'Therefore a man shall leave his father and his mother and hold fast to his wife, and the two shall become one flesh'? So they are no longer two but one flesh. What therefore God has joined together, let not man separate." (Matt. 19:4–6)

THE FIRST FLOOR

Biblical Truths

- God created all people boys and girls (male and female) (Gen. 1:26–28).
- God loves boys and girls exactly the same.
- We cannot change the things that make us a boy or a girl.

- Usually, there are "boy" things and "girl" things: boys like to play with trucks and trains while girls like to play with dolls and kitchens. It is good to be a boy and play with boy things. It is good to be a girl and play with girl things. But if you're a boy who likes to play with kitchens, that does not make you a girl. And if you're a girl who likes to play with trucks, that does not make you a boy.
- We can grow up to be anything we want (a doctor, a teacher, a plumber), but we will never be able to change from a man into a woman or a woman into a man.

Conversation Starters

- Who created all people?
- What kind of people did God create?
- Does God love boys and girls the same?
- Can you change the things that make you a boy or girl?
- What happens if you like playing with a "boy" thing or a "girl" thing?
- What can you grow up to be? Can you choose to become either a man or a woman?

THE SECOND FLOOR
Biblical Truths

- God created all people either male or female (Gen. 1:26–28).
- God gave males and females different, specific jobs: our physical bodies are designed differently for the purpose of having children.

- God loves males and females equally, but he gives us separate roles and abilities: males (fathers) are typically strong and protective, while females (mothers) are typically caring and nurturing.
- We cannot change our maleness or femaleness.
- Cultures often define what is appropriate for "boys" and "girls" to do or play. In our culture, we see boys do things like play sports, hunt, and build things. We see girls do things like dance, perform in the theater, and cook. It is good for us to follow the appropriate pathways that our culture considers "masculine" and "feminine" as they help us see how boys and girls are different. But sometimes, a boy may like to cook or dance, and a girl may like to hunt or build furniture. Doing something that the culture deems only appropriate for the opposite gender does not make you less of a "boy" or a "girl." Even if you like "boy" things or "girl" things, you cannot, and will never be able to, change your God-given maleness or femaleness assigned to you at conception.

Conversation Starters

- How many kinds of people did God create? Who are they?
- What specific jobs did God give males and females? How are they different from one another?
- How did God create males and females equally? Separately?
- Why can we not change our maleness and femaleness?
- What does it mean to like "boy" things or "girl" things? Why does that still not change our maleness and femaleness? Have you ever thought about wanting to change your maleness or femaleness?

THE THIRD FLOOR

Biblical Truths

- God created male and female and assigned male and female at conception (Gen. 1:26–28).
- Males and females are identified by unique bodily characteristics designed purposefully for reproduction and earthly dominion (Gen. 1:28).
- Following biblical sexuality is recognizing that the male and female bodies are designed in reciprocal and complementary ways. Proper actions are natural and honoring to God. Improper actions of the body are immoral.
- While God sees males and females as equal in worth and dignity, he gives us unique gifts that we demonstrate in masculine and feminine ways: males (fathers) are typically strong and protective, while females (mothers) are typically more caring and nurturing.
- Gender is rooted in biological sex. You are first and foremost male or female because of your body. You show the world your maleness or femaleness through your gender norms.
- Cultures guide what is appropriate for males and females. It is good for us to follow these cultural gender norms, as they maintain differences between genders. But failure to adhere to *all* of a culture's gender norms does not change your maleness or femaleness. It is okay if you do not fit every cultural stereotype of your gender. You are not any less male or female. You are a male or female because of your body. You are not a male or female strictly because of your culture's gender norms or your feelings.

- Male and female are not cultural constructs that can become fluid or be changed. Being male or female is embedded in realities knit into the creation order.

Conversation Starters

- How does God assign and differentiate male and female? What is God's command to us? How are our bodies an important part of that command?
- What is biblical sexuality? Why is it important to have a firm understanding of true biblical sexuality? Where does the moral and immoral conversation fit? Have you encountered this conversation with friends?
- What is the same and different about males and females? Have you seen this true in your father and mother? Any other examples?
- What do you think it means for male and female to be equal in worth and dignity but separate in function? Why is that an important distinction?
- Why does each culture drive the actions, tendencies, and appearances for the males and females in that place and time of history? What stereotypes have you seen? Do you feel the pressure to live up to any particular stereotypes? Do you have friends caught in this right now? How can you help them see the truth?
- Culture today tells us that you can be anyone you want to be any day or time you decide, that gender is fluid and can be changed. What do you think about that? Have you ever struggled with your maleness or femaleness? Do you have any friends who are struggling with their maleness

or femaleness right now? How can you talk with friends about being male and female as part of the way the world naturally works, even if they don't believe in God? How can we (your parents) help you? How can we (your parents) help your friends?

RECOMMENDED RESOURCES

Allison, Gregg R. *Embodied: Living as Whole People in a Fractured World*. Grand Rapids, MI: Baker, 2021.

Burk, Denny, Colin Smothers, and David Closson, *Male and Female He Created Them: A Study on Gender, Sexuality, and Marriage*. Fearn, UK: Christian Focus, 2023.

Clark, Stephen B. *Man and Woman in Christ: An Examination of the Roles of Men and Women in Light of Scripture and the Social Sciences*. Bloomington, IN: Warhorn Media, 2021.

Favale, Abigail. *The Genesis of Gender: A Christian Theory*. San Francisco: Ignatius, 2022.

Köstenberger, Andreas J., and Margaret E. Köstenberger, *God's Design for Man and Woman: A Biblical-Theological Survey*. Wheaton, IL: Crossway, 2014.

Piper, John, and Wayne Grudem, *Recovering Biblical Manhood and Womanhood: A Response to Evangelical Feminism*. Wheaton, IL: Crossway, 2021.

5

Homosexuality

WE AREN'T IN A REVOLUTION. The revolution has now passed. It's unfathomable in today's culture that any elite individual or institution would speak critically of homosexuality. From the time we graduated college (2008) to today, perspectives around sexuality—particularly if you live in a more politically progressive area—have completely flipped.

No issue may be more divisive and delicate than this one. Everyone likely knows and loves someone who may identify as LGBTQ+. As parents, we know you're trying to foster a balance between loving those you genuinely care for while also being un-flinchingly faithful to what the Bible says about homosexuality. We know you're trying to walk what seems like a teeter-totter between grace and truth. Scripture says grace and truth were present in equal measure in Jesus (John 1:14). We think they can be present in equal measure for you too.

I still remember when I (Andrew) had to talk to our oldest daughter about homosexuality. I forget what occasioned it, but

I remember her being at an age where I needed to say *something*. Given her age, I vividly recall saying, "Well, Caroline, there are people who think that it is okay for two men or two women to be married to one another." Caroline had a confused look on her face. I went on to tell her, "Even though we can be kind to everyone, your mom and I don't believe that is God's plan for marriage. God's plan for marriage is one man, one woman, and their babies." Being the young age she was, she did not press further at the time and went on to the next thing. The biggest challenge and need was for me to say something, anything really, that would satisfy the moment.

BIBLICAL TEACHING OVERVIEW

As we think about *how we think about* the issues, it's important to differentiate between complexity and controversy. There are positions that Christians hold that are controversial but not all that complex. This is one of those issues. Speaking as someone (Andrew) who studies the issues professionally, if there is any topic where Christian interpretation and Christian history have been consistently aligned, it is the immorality of homosexuality. Remember from chapter 3 that the Bible's teaching on sexuality is governed by a logic established within creation order itself: the complementary design of man and woman is what makes them, and them *alone*, suited for marriage. The Genesis formula is at the heart of this design:

God creates humanity. →
    God creates humanity male and female. →
        God makes male and female for one another
            (Gen. 1:26–28; 2:18–24).

As we said in a previous chapter, it bears repeating again: the logic of bodily sex difference helps explain the moral logic of biblical sexual ethics overall. The mandate for sexual relations in Scripture is tied to the design of the body. The logic and good of marriage is tied to the design of those bodies. Male and female bodies are designed for one another in a reciprocal complementary and life-giving way. We understand what biblical sexuality is by respecting the natural design of the body. The end for which the body is organized—namely, reproduction—tells us what sexual actions are proper to the body and which actions are immoral. While seeking to be honest in how we depict same-sex sexual activity, same-sex sexual activity signals a misuse of the body since homosexual acts thwart or work against the natural purpose of sexual design. In female same-sex sexual acts, the result is fruitless sex since reproduction is thwarted. In male same-sex sexual acts, the result is the same: fruitless, non-reproductive sex that damages the body's design.

Everywhere homosexuality is mentioned in the Bible, it is mentioned critically. I (Andrew) have heard it repeated more than I can count that because homosexuality is mentioned so sparsely, the Bible does not put that big of a focus on it, so why should we? For one, statements like this are evidence of a bad approach to biblical interpretation. If we are called to obey something in Scripture—even once—we are to obey Scripture. We do not get to pick and choose what we obey based on numerical frequency. That is not how biblical ethics is done. Two, considering that the Bible's prohibitions on homosexuality are set against a creational backdrop that governs the whole narrative of Scripture, there need not be, nor should one expect there to be, hundreds of verses of condemnation. The sparseness at which homosexuality is mentioned is actually an affirmation of God's creational pattern and confirmation of Scripture's abiding condemnation of all sexual practices that transgress God's instructions. Approving homosexual activity abandons scriptural authority, and all who belong to Christ are to obey his words (John 14:15–31).

The Bible prohibits all forms of homosexuality. The Bible's condemnation of homosexuality is a comprehensive condemnation. Often it is said by revisionist and progressive voices that Scripture is only prohibiting homosexual relations that are inherently exploitative or abusive. So the argument goes: if the authors of Scripture knew of loving and monogamous same-sex relationships, they wouldn't condemn them. The problem is that Scripture recognizes no such distinction because Scripture speaks categorically in blanket opposition to all forms of homosexual activity because all homosexual activity—done in whatever context—violates God's creational blueprint (Rom. 1:18–32). Whether consensual or monogamous, same-sex sexual activity is still gravely sinful and immoral (1 Cor. 6:9–10). Scripture presents no circumstance where homosexual activity of any kind is morally appropriate.

The Bible's prohibition on homosexuality is grounded in creational reality. The prohibitions against homosexual activity are not arbitrary or oppressive. The prohibitions reflect the normative reality that sexuality's ultimate purpose is not pleasure for pleasure's own sake, but reproductive ability. Were it not for the creational blueprint upholding the primacy of reproduction as the basis for sexual activity, it is questionable whether there would be sexuality at all.

After all, what would be the point of sexual attraction if individuals could spawn offspring on their own? Where Scripture speaks of sexuality, it is purposeful sexuality for the sake of propagating human populations and the cultivation of cultural order. Scripture thus speaks of a fixed creation order where certain actions accord with this order, and others do not. Hence, in Romans 1:18–32, where Paul speaks most sweepingly against homosexuality, it is done against a fixed backdrop where it is considered "contrary to nature" for bodies to be used in opposition to their natural design (Rom. 1:26). The "nature" Scripture speaks of are the creational laws that beckon us to honor the natural design of our bodies.

Jesus affirms the immorality of homosexuality. Like our discussion around gender and sexuality, the New Testament and Jesus himself affirm the abiding validity of Genesis's creational blueprint. In Matthew 19:4–6, Jesus upholds the complementarity of the sexes within the marriage covenant as the exclusive ground for sexual activity. Furthermore, Jesus's condemnation of *porneia* (Mark 7:21) is a condemnation of any form of non-marital intercourse, which would necessarily include homosexual activity.

Claiming an identity at odds with Scripture is never fulfilling. We understand that for many people, this topic, perhaps more than any other, pulls at the heartstrings. You may be internally thinking to yourself, "This is just who people are, and they deserve to be happy and fulfilled in who they are." We understand the appeal of this logic. After all, who isn't in favor of people being happy? But we have to challenge this thinking with the authority of Scripture. Underneath this sentiment is a mistaken understanding of contentment and happiness.

Scripture posits no reality where living contrary to God's word, in the long run, prospers individuals. In addition to eternal judgment, no individual can run against the grain of the Creator's universe and expect to flourish. Individuals might suppress the truth in unrighteousness or deceive themselves into thinking they are happy (Rom. 1:18; Heb. 3:13), but we cannot rest content in moral indifference if we truly love people. We are to love our neighbor as ourselves (Mark 12:30–31), and one way we love our neighbors is by giving them the truth they are owed (1 Cor. 13:6), which is the most loving thing that can be shared, regardless of the difficulty. We are to walk in the light and put off all sexual immorality (Col. 3:5–10; 1 John 1:7).

Expect and prepare for disagreement. Many times, people approach me (Andrew) with the underlying assumption that if they answer a person's question with incredible charity and kindness, then they will not face criticism. That's desirable, of course, but our call to do good to outsiders in even the most charitable and respectful of ways is no promise that we will escape criticism or even persecution (2 Tim. 3:12). We are commanded to do well to outsiders because Scripture commands it (Col. 4:5–6), not because it promises to remove us from uncomfortable situations. If Jesus faced opposition, we are not beneath experiencing what he did as well (Matt. 10:22; John 15:18). Remember, above all: You are never "on the wrong side of history" if you are on the right side of God's word.

———

Here are some basic biblical, theological, and philosophical truths that every parent should know:

- Every human being is sexually broken and in equal need of redemption.
- God loves sexual sinners and died to redeem them.
- Every human being is worthy of respect and kindness.
- Every human being is owed the truth.
- Grace and truth should never be in conflict.
- The Bible's sexual ethic has an internal logic to its consistency. If it is rejected, further sexual boundary-breaking will always ensue.
- If the moral ideal governing sexuality is anything short of marriage, it is virtually impossible to disapprove of any sexual practice or sexual identity on principle.
- The connective tissue that explains conflicts over gender, marriage, and sexuality is the false ideology that human nature has no fixed identity or purpose.
- Indulging sexual desire apart from marriage may bring short-term gratification, but a pattern of sexual sin is unfulfilling and personally and culturally destructive.
- We must remember that every single human being is searching for peace, contentment, and happiness. Only Christ can ultimately satisfy those longings.
- We must prepare ourselves for insult and persecution over this issue.
- No parent should feel pressured to cut off contact with a child who identifies as LGBTQ+.[1]

---

1   This is a topic deserving of more space than we can provide. The position we hold to is that a child's sin does not erase the fact that the child in question is still a beloved child of his or her parents. Scripture never teaches that a child's sin requires abandonment. Wisdom requires handling each situation uniquely. This, of course,

NOTE: Homosexuality and transgenderism are sensitive and awkward topics to discuss with your children of any age. Start talking to them at young ages and encourage them to come to you about ANYTHING. You want them to trust you, and you want them to share things with you. As they share what they hear, what their friends are going through, what they see, etc., be prepared for some things you may not want to hear. Stay calm and try not to react in a negative way.

We all must also remember that kids are complex and they are sinners. They will do stupid things. They will disappoint us. They may even rebel against us. Make sure they know and are reminded over and over again that your love for them is not dependent on their behavior. If they begin to struggle with same-sex attraction or are questioning their gender, continue to love them with grace and truth. There is room for them to grow and mature. Let them know that the Lord is capable of transforming them. Above all else, continue to disciple them. Pray for them. Love them.

MEMORY VERSE

Or do you not know that the unrighteous will not inherit the kingdom of God? Do not be deceived: neither the sexually immoral, nor idolaters, nor adulterers, nor men who practice homosexuality, nor thieves, nor the greedy, nor drunkards, nor revilers, nor swindlers will inherit the kingdom of God. And such were some of you. But you were washed, you were

does not mean affirming a child's sin, but that a child remains your child even if in unrepentant sin.

sanctified, you were justified in the name of the Lord Jesus Christ and by the Spirit of our God. (1 Cor. 6:9–11)

THE FIRST FLOOR

Biblical Truths

- All Scripture is true and breathed out by God (2 Tim. 3:16).
- We are to obey all that God wrote in Scripture (John 14:15).
- God created boys and girls to grow up to maybe become a husband or a wife and maybe become a dad and a mom to any children that God gives them. Every boy and girl needs a daddy and a mommy (Gen. 1:26–28).
- Every boy and girl is a sinner who disobeys God's commands. We need Jesus to save us from our sin. Only Jesus, God's Son, came to earth to live a perfect life, died on the cross for our sins, was buried, and rose from the dead on the third day. If you confess your sin and believe that Jesus was God's Son, you will be saved (Rom. 10:9–10).
- Every boy and girl was created by God and deserves kindness and respect (Matt. 22:37–39).

Conversation Starters

- What is Scripture? Is it *all* true? Who wrote the Bible?
- Should we obey *some* Scripture or *all* Scripture? Why?
- Who created boys and girls? What will boys and girls become when they grow up? What might God give

some husbands and wives? What does every boy and girl need?

- What does it mean to be a sinner? Who is the only person who can save us? How?
- Who created every boy and girl? What does every boy and girl deserve? How can we show kindness to our friends? How can we show respect to our friends?

THE SECOND FLOOR
Biblical Truths

- All Scripture is true and written by chosen men who were inspired by the Holy Spirit (2 Tim. 3:16).
- We are called to obey all Scripture. We do not get to pick and choose which parts of Scripture we like or want to obey (John 14:15).
- God created men and women to be husbands and wives and to be fathers and mothers to any children God may give them. God made men and women differently so they can provide different needs for their children (like fathers provide protection and mothers are uniquely gentle). Children need a father and a mother (Gen. 1:26–28; 2:18–24).
- Every human is a sinner who disobeys God's commands. We need Jesus to save us from our sin. Only Jesus, God's Son, came to earth to live a perfect life, died on the cross for our sins, was buried, and rose from the dead on the third day. If you confess your sin and believe that Jesus was God's Son, you will be saved (Rom. 10:9–10).

- Every human is owed kindness and respect because every human is made in the image of God (Matt. 22:37–39).
- We are to speak the truth of Scripture to others in equal measures of grace and truth (1 Cor. 13:6).

Conversation Starters

- What parts of Scripture are true? Who wrote the Bible?
- What parts of Scripture are we called to obey? What if we don't like what some parts of the Bible say?
- Who did God create? How many different kinds of humans did God create? What does God intend boys and girls to grow up to become? Do children need a dad and a mom? How are dads and moms different? What might happen if a child has two dads and no mom or two moms and no dad? How will that affect the child as he or she grows up? Do you know anyone with two dads or two moms?
- Why does every human need Jesus? How can we be saved from our sin? Do you have friends who need to hear about Jesus? How can we help you tell them?
- What do we owe every human? Why?
- What is grace? What is truth? Why do we have a responsibility to tell others the truth of Scripture with both grace *and* truth?

THE THIRD FLOOR

Biblical Truths

- Biblical inerrancy means that all Scripture is without error or fault. God wrote the Bible through chosen men who were inspired by the Holy Spirit (2 Tim. 3:16).

- Biblical ethics requires us to obey all Scripture because Scripture is true and breathed out by God. The Bible is not a buffet line of things we choose to obey because they are fun, easy, or fit with our lifestyles. God is holy and righteous, his word tells us how to live in a holy and righteous way, and we are to follow all of his commands. Some people might say that homosexuality is okay because the Bible only speaks against it a few times. But whether the Bible commands something once or a hundred times, we are to obey it all the same (John 14:15).

- Biblical sexuality shows that God created male and female bodies to be complementary to one another. The bodily designs show that the purpose of reproduction is central to our bodies' design. Homosexuality is in opposition to the natural order of creation that honors the design of our bodies (Gen. 1:26–28; Rom. 1:18–32).

- God created men and women to be husbands and wives and fathers and mothers to any children God may give them. Children need a father and a mother, and the differences they each bring to the home. Homosexual families can provide care, but not the fully functioning marriage and family situation that is needed for children to thrive.

- Every human is a sinner in need of a Savior. Every human is broken in his or her sexuality and in need of redemption. Only Jesus can save sinners and provide redemption through his life, death, and resurrection (Rom. 10:9–10).
- Every one of us will encounter a friend, family member, or neighbor that is struggling or will struggle with homosexuality. Every person was created in the image of God and deserves kindness and respect. Everyone is longing for peace, contentment, and happiness. Only Christ can satisfy those things.
- Every human is owed the truth of the gospel of Jesus Christ. We should speak in equal measure of both grace and truth (Matt. 22:37–39).
- As we love those around us and speak the truth of Scripture, we should expect to encounter insults and persecution (John 15:20).

Conversation Starters

- What is biblical inerrancy? What is Scripture? Why can it be trusted?
- What is biblical ethics? How much Scripture do we obey? Why? Why would some people try to only obey parts of Scripture? What could we say to those people?
- What is biblical sexuality? How do we know men and women are created for each other? How does homosexuality go against that created order? How does it violate God's plan for marriage and family?
- What is the natural order for men and women as they grow up? How are they different? How are your dad and

mom different? Why is it important for children to have both a dad and a mom? How would children be affected negatively if they had two dads or two moms?

- How does sexual sin break you? How does Jesus provide salvation and redemption? Have you been saved from your sin? Do you have sexual brokenness (same-sex attraction, pornography, etc.)? How can we (your parents) help you?

- Do you know anyone struggling with same-sex attraction right now? How have you shown him or her kindness and respect? If you haven't, how can you show kindness and respect? Do you see in him or her a longing for peace, contentment, or happiness? What is he or she doing to find that longing fulfilled in other things instead of Christ? How can we (your parents) help you help him or her?

- What do you think it means that every human is "owed the truth"? What is grace? What is truth? How do we speak those in equal measure?

- Have you ever been insulted or persecuted for speaking the truth? (Parents, if you have been insulted or persecuted, share your story with your kids so they don't feel alone.)

RECOMMENDED RESOURCES

Allberry, Sam. *Is God Anti-Gay? And Other Questions about Jesus, the Bible, and Same-Sex Sexuality*. Epsom, UK: The Good Book Company, 2015.

DeYoung, Kevin. *What Does the Bible Really Teach about Homosexuality?* Wheaton, IL: Crossway, 2015.

Forston, S. Donald, and Rollin G. Grams, *Unchanging Witness: The Consistent Christian Teaching on Homosexuality in Scripture and Tradition*. Nashville, TN: B&H Academic, 2016.

Gagnon, Robert. *The Bible and Homosexual Practice: Texts and Hermeneutics*. Nashville, TN: Abingdon, 2001.

6

Identity

IN AN INFAMOUS 1992 Supreme Court ruling that reaffirmed the "right"[1] to abortion in the United States Constitution, Justice Anthony Kennedy used a phrase to justify abortion that many consider to be one of the most important quotes for understanding modern culture. According to Justice Anthony Kennedy, "At the heart of liberty is the right to define one's own concept of existence, of meaning, of the universe, and of the mystery of human life."[2]

Note what is central to Kennedy's statement: the *individual* possesses total sovereignty to determine for him- or herself what

1   It is our settled view that there is no legal or moral right to an abortion. Abortion is nowhere in the text of the Constitution and moreover, the right to one's existence given by God should preclude any provision for one to be legally murdered. Biblically speaking, there is no moral right to do evil, either. While governments will rightfully determine what degree of wrongdoing it will permit before punishment is deemed necessary, it is our conviction that the Bible's prohibition on murder and the logic of homicide laws preclude there ever being a moral right to an abortion.
2   Planned Parenthood of Southeastern PA v. Casey, 505 U.S. 833, 851 (1992), https://supreme.justia.com.

is right and wrong. Some scholars refer to this pronounced emphasis on the human person being at the center of his or her own universe as "expressive individualism." One scholar defines expressive individualism as the

> desire to pursue one's own path but also a yearning for fulfillment through the definition and articulation of one's own identity. It is a drive both to be more like whatever you already are and also to live in society by fully asserting who you are. The capacity of individuals to define the terms of their own existence by defining their personal identities is increasingly equated with liberty and with the meaning of some of our basic rights, and it is given pride of place in our self-understanding.[3]

This is the central ethic that guides our society's thinking in contemporary America. The idea that a person would be limited by an authority outside of him- or herself—whether a tradition, religion, or parent—to do or experience whatever he or she wants amounts to one of the worst offenses an authority can commit.

The question we should immediately ask ourselves is whether expressive individualism can be consistently lived out. Of course, it cannot be. We do not look on at monsters like Adolf Hitler and say, "Hey man, you do you. Live your truth." No one in their right mind would defend Hitler, but then that same person will turn around and defend the rights of others to perceive themselves how they want to be perceived or identify. The way to explain this contradiction is to understand that our society bestows legitimacy

3   Yuval Levin, *The Fractured Republic: Renewing America's Social Contract in the Age of Individualism* (New York: Basic, 2016), 148.

on whatever "identity" someone wants insofar as there aren't obvious harms attached to it. But then that raises a question: Who gets to define what a harm is?

For example, a few years ago it was discovered that a Caucasian woman, Rachel Dolezal, was identifying as an African American woman. There was justifiable outrage—but only because she claimed an "identity" that did not square with reality. But then our society turns around and praises men who want to identify as women.

The focus on "identity" leads to cascading moral confusion. Some can claim an "identity" as a way to insulate themselves against critique. After all, the thinking goes in our age: if morality is relative, who is to say any identity is, in fact, wrong? What are the moral criteria for judging some identities as okay and others not?

When compared to previous generations, what is unique about the modern age is our culture's fascination and obsession with "identity." The search for identity is not plausible apart from other realities in our culture, namely, the ideas of self-actualization, therapeutic affirmation, and moral relativism. Assuring that someone's feelings are not hurt but rather affirmed appears to be the highest good to which our society aspires. This pronounced focus on the *Self* as the thing that must be satisfied above all has led to an age of coddling, fragility, and moral confusion.

What Christians should be most interested in getting answers to is really just two questions: Who owns us? Who defines what is good for us? There are only two options: (1) a secular view where identity and goodness are self-determined; or (2) a Christian view where identity and goodness are God-determined.

BIBLICAL TEACHING OVERVIEW

Now, before being critical of *how* our society fixates on identity, it's necessary to consider whether there may be a deeply biblical impulse at the heart of this search for identity. We think there is. We are convinced that it is Christianity that best satisfies people's need for identity, but it is the eclipse of Christianity by secularism that is producing a stream of identities that is leading people astray.

Individuals are made to know God. Augustine famously said that "our hearts are restless until they find their rest in thee [God]."[4] Knowing God as our heavenly Father bestows on humanity our crowning identity as image-bearers made to derive our ultimate sense of worth from him.

From a theological perspective, there is an explanation for this phenomenon. When the world collapses in on itself and removes transcendence as the explanation for the origins of life, morality, and ultimate purpose, something will fill that void. The question is *which* paradigm will inform our identity, not *whether* one will.

The Bible provides a comprehensive and stable account of human identity. The centerpiece for determining identity begins with the fact of God making humanity in his image (Gen. 1:26–28). Genesis provides the essential building blocks to understand who we are and what we are made for: (1) we exist as persons for whom life itself is valuable for its own sake; (2) we are made in God's

---

4 Augustine, *Confessions*, trans. Henry Chadwick (Oxford: Oxford University Press, 1991), 3.

image as either male or female; and (3) our existence as males and females allows us to form families and build cultures for the sake of God's glory. Existence, identity, and family are essential building blocks for rooting one's sense of place in the world. As we discussed in the chapter on human dignity (chapter 1), the image of God confers dignity, moral duty, and the ultimate reference point for understanding who we are. God providentially creates us (Psalm 139), cares for us (Matt. 6:26), and appoints where it is we will live (Acts 17:26). Knowing God is where our souls are meant to find rest and contentment.

We are not made in our parents' image or the culture's image, ultimately. We are not the product of blind chance. The most important fact of our existence from the perspective of Christianity is that God is our Creator. If we put our focus on anything apart from God to derive a sense of self-worth, imitators will always deceive and disappoint.

Biblical love does not mean affirming non-biblical identities. Loving your neighbor as yourself does not mean uncritically affirming or accepting whatever "identity" your neighbor wants affirmed (Mark 12:30–31). To love your friends properly is to give your friends what they are owed: truth. Truth is always a healing balm, even if rejected. Love rejoices in the truth (1 Cor. 13:6), and regardless of whether your friends or neighbors interpret your actions or words as loving, Christians must always operate from that motivation.

Moral relativism at the level of personal identity is unsustainable and harmful. Though it appears loving and tolerant to simply affirm whatever identity someone adopts for himself, we must see the barrage of possible identities as what it truly is: destabilizing. Human nature is not meant to wrestle with existential questions of identity apart from God's authority. To insist that every individual is responsible for searching and arriving at his or her own personal identity is a burden too heavy to carry. The Bible condemns situations where "everyone did what was right in his own eyes" (Judg. 21:25). Apart from the Bible, there is no limiting principle that prevents individuals from adopting absurd conclusions about their identities. Where unbelief and secularism provide an endless search, Scripture makes the audacious claim that who we are is *not* mystery. Jesus calls all people—even those exhausted in the search for significance—to come to him for rest (Matt. 11:28). Our identity is meant to be received from God, not constructed by human autonomy.

The Bible provides a consistent and impartial standard for judging which identities are sinful and which are morally good. One criticism of Christianity in consideration of identity is the accusation that Christians are hateful, hypocritical, or arbitrary in what identities they condemn or affirm. Sure, Christians can be hateful, hypocritical, or arbitrary. But that is a failure of individual Christians, not of biblical Christianity. Christianity is not a moral free-for-all. Christians subscribe to the Bible as their highest authority. So considerations about what is right or wrong is not up to individual Christians. Moral judgments flow from what the Bible teaches regarding the moral question at hand. It is often alleged that Christians are not to judge others (Matt. 7:1–2). The Bible's admonition is not the suspension of moral judgment but the application of impartial judgment. At the end of the day, even proponents of expressive individualism draw the moral line somewhere in what is or isn't a proper identity. It's a question of where the lines are drawn and whether they are drawn arbitrarily or not.

There are other identity-giving forces in our lives, but none as important as God. Scripture is not opposed to human identity being formed by other realities insofar as those realities are interpreted in light of Scripture. For example, the fact of nationality, family origin, and tradition are not, on the surface, inherently unbiblical aspects of forming a human identity. These are important constituent pieces of the puzzle in forming one's identity. People do not have to turn their backs on their homelands or their families in order to know God. Those realities must be subordinated to the highest reality that shapes identity: God.

———

Here are some basic biblical, theological, and philosophical truths every Christian parent should know:

- The image of God is the foundation for human identity.
- The search for identity, while problematic when taken to the extreme, must be seen as a God-given impulse meant for us to find our identity ultimately in him.
- Apart from Scripture, humanity will search in vain for identities that will satisfy.

- One of the assumptions of Scripture is that the identity given to us by God as image-bearers is meant to address fundamental questions of human existence: Where did we come from? Who are we? What is our purpose? What is truth? Scripture grounds the answers to these questions theocentrically (with God at the center), not anthropocentrically (with humans at the center).

- At the heart of questions around identity are questions of where we place our foundation for trust and authority.

- Human beings cannot bear the weight of endlessly wrestling and searching after their identities apart from God.

- Modern fixation with identity cannot provide a definitive foundation for who we are.

- Modern ideas around identity do not have consistent limiting principles.

MEMORY VERSE

Know that the Lord, he is God!
   It is he who made us, and we are his;
   we are his people, and the sheep of his pasture. (Ps. 100:3)

THE FIRST FLOOR

Biblical Truths

- God is King and Ruler (Psalm 47).
- God created all people in his image (Gen. 1:26–28).

- God created all people for his glory (Psalm 8).
- God made you to be exactly who you are on purpose and and he has a plan for your life (Ps. 32:8; Rom. 8:28).
- We can trust God because his word is true and he always keeps his promises (Prov. 3:5–6).

Conversation Starters

- Who is God? What does he rule over?
- Who did God create? What does it mean to be created in his image?
- Why did God create us for his glory? How can we bring glory to God?
- How does God care for people? How does God care for you?
- What are some specific ways that God created you special, unlike anyone else?
- How do you know you can trust God? Does God keep his promises?

THE SECOND FLOOR

Biblical Truths

- God is King and the ultimate authority in this world (Psalm 47).
- God created all people in his image (Gen. 1:26–28).
- Our identity is found in God, not in ourselves. God is truth, we are not (John 8:32; 14:6).

- Scripture answers the questions about our identity: where we came from, who we are, our purpose in life, and the definition of truth.
- God's blueprint in Genesis provides our purpose (Gen. 1:26–28):
  - our life has dignity and value
  - we are created male and female in God's image
  - as males and females, we can build families to bring God glory
- God created you exactly how he wanted you. He has a plan and purpose for your life (Ps. 16:9; Rom. 8:28).

Conversation Starters

- Who is the ultimate authority in this world? What does that mean?
- What does it mean to be created in God's image? Who is created in his image?
- What is identity? Do we get to define our own concept of existence or identity? How is God truth? Why can we trust him to be true? Can you trust yourself or your feelings to be true?
- How does Scripture answer questions about our identity? Can you trust Scripture to be true?
- How does Genesis provide an outline of God's purpose for people? What does it mean for life to have dignity and value? How does building families bring God glory?
- Do you believe that God created you and you matter to him? Have you ever had feelings that you don't like who you are or that you aren't good enough? How can we (your

parents) help you? Have you seen God working any plans or purposes in your life?

THE THIRD FLOOR

Biblical Truths

- God is the Alpha and Omega. God is the only authority that has been, is, and will be, now and forever, in this world (Psalm 47).
- God created male and female in his image. We are the only part of his creation that bears his likeness morally, spiritually, and intellectually. Recognizing that we are his image-bearers is the foundation of human identity (Gen. 1:26–28).
- Our identities are given by God and rooted in God's truth. Our identities cannot be rooted in ourselves because the self is deceitful. The burden of finding and determining our own identities is too big a burden for us to carry outside of God's truth and authority (John 8:32; 14:6).
- Scripture grounds identity in God and provides us with purpose. Scripture answers the questions of identity: where we came from, who we are, our purpose in life, and the definition of truth. God's natural plan of creation provides our purpose in Genesis: our life has value, God created us male and female, and many males and females are called to be husbands and wives and fathers and mothers to any children that their union produces. This is how we bring glory to God.

- You have been created exactly as God designed. He gave you the very physical, spiritual, and intellectual qualities he wanted you to possess. There is no one else like you in this world. He has a specific plan and purpose for your life using the very gifts he gave you at your creation. Your outward or inward identity cannot be separated from God's design (Ps. 32:8; Rom. 8:28).
- Biblical love does not affirm non-biblical identities. As Christians, we cannot affirm self-proclaimed identities that are separated from God's image, truth, and authority. Biblical love requires us to love others and speak God's truth to them with an equal measure of grace and truth (1 Cor. 13:6).

Conversation Starters

- This world falls under whose authority? For how long has this world been under God's authority? Why do you think some people disregard God's authority? Do you think the authority of "self" is a better authority than God? Have you ever had problems trusting God's authority? Where will you place your trust and authority?
- How are humans created in the image of God? How do humans bear his likeness? How is this the foundation of human identity?
- How is identity given by God and rooted in God's truth? How can the "self" be deceitful? Why does the possibility of the self being deceitful make it unreliable to root identity in the self? How is determining our own identity a burden? Why would that be too big a burden outside of God's truth and authority?

- How does Scripture ground identity and provide purpose? What questions of identity does Scripture answer? How does God's plan of creation in Genesis provide our purpose? How does God's natural plan bring him glory? What happens if you try to find your identity apart from what Scripture teaches?

- Do you truly believe that God created you to be exactly what he wanted you to be? What are your favorite physical, spiritual, and intellectual qualities God gave you? What special gifts and skills did God create in you? Do you believe God has a plan and purpose for your life? Have your feelings ever deceived you? Have you ever wanted to change who you are? How can we (your parents) help you?

- What is a biblical identity? What is a non-biblical identity? Can you affirm non-biblical identity? How does the Bible require you to love others struggling with their identities? Have you ever struggled with your identity? How can we (your parents) help you? Do you have friends who struggle with their identities? How can you talk to them about biblical identity?

RECOMMENDED RESOURCES

Bridges, Jerry. *Who Am I? Identity in Christ*. Minneapolis: Cruciform Press, 2012.

Lewis, C. S. *The Abolition of Man*. New York: HarperCollins, 1944.

Schaeffer, Francis. *How Should We Then Live?* Wheaton, IL: Crossway, 1976, 2021.

Sire, James. *The Universe Next Door: A Basic Worldview Catalog.* Downers Grove, IL: InterVarsity Press, 1976, 1997.

Trueman, Carl R. *The Rise and Triumph of the Modern Self: Cultural Amnesia, Expressive Individualism, and the Road to Sexual Revolution.* Wheaton, IL: Crossway, 2020.

7

Transgenderism

I (ANDREW) HAD FINISHED speaking at a church on a Sunday night, and a line of people formed to ask me questions. Since I write, teach, and speak about a lot of controversial topics, I've grown accustomed to people asking me really difficult questions about many topics.

A lady approached me, a little frantic. I listened attentively as she asked my advice on what she should do to help her teenage nephew, who was considering drastic and invasive "transition" procedures to allow him to live as a woman. She told me that he came from a broken family and that one of the parents had come out as gay. The teenager had lived as a girl since early adolescence and was always emotionally fragile and socially awkward. The child had been on puberty blockers and was undergoing hormone therapies. It was obvious this woman loved her nephew. There was no anger, only desperation.

A similar conversation took place over the phone. A woman called my office phone and told me that her daughter, who had always had a rebellious streak though generally a normal child, was beginning to "transition." She explained that she had begun spending hours on YouTube watching other teens document their transitions. The girl was influenced by what she saw and, enthralled at the possibility of online attention, she started a YouTube channel. Sure enough, the teenage girl would eventually go on to question whether she was, in fact, truly a girl. The mother was, understandably, distraught.

Both of these situations perfectly capture the volatility, vulnerability, and deceit at the heart of the transgender movement. What began as a movement centered upon individuals who report genuine distress about their bodies and minds seeming at odds, has metastasized far beyond the search for self-acceptance. Gender ideology has been weaponized by the combination of broken families, mental health challenges, and cultural forces that glamorize questioning one's identity.

In a previous chapter, we looked at what the Bible says positively about gender (chapter 4). In this chapter, we will explore an issue at odds with the Bible's concept of gender—transgenderism, the movement that has accelerated more briskly in culture than any other in American history. It is also the movement showing the greatest signs of internal exhaustion and looming collapse.

BIBLICAL TEACHING OVERVIEW

An anchor of this book has been the bedrock foundation that Genesis 1–2 provides for the Christian worldview. It is not an overstatement to suggest that most of today's most controversial subjects all share a common feature of trying to assault the worldview of Genesis 1. Those chapters factor so heavily into our thinking about everyday life because Genesis 1–2 builds the stage where our lives and existence unfold. The Genesis formula provides fertile ground for establishing the fact of our existence, a concrete identity, and the centrality of the family. Essential to the Genesis worldview is the reality and givenness of sex difference. That is where all conversations around gender and transgenderism must begin. The fundamental distinction in classifying human beings is the body's form and organization—not skin color, ethnicity, intelligence, or whatever else.

Sex difference is an embodied reality. The Bible depicts humankind as comprised of two distinct sexes—male and female. To be male is not, first and foremost, to embody certain cultural expressions, like wearing blue. To be male or female is to possess a male or female body. Our bodies are not blank canvasses. There is a purpose to the design that our bodies exhibit. That purpose, fundamentally, is the body's organization for reproduction. That is the only stable way to define male and female. Any other classifications are built off that primary foundation.

As we've stressed, male and female are unchanging categories defined by the body's organization for reproduction. That may sound a bit technical, so think of it this way: To identify what X *is*, you have to know what it is *for*. To know what X is *for*, one must understand the composite parts that make X work to their predetermined purpose. Our body's design is a signpost to understanding what our bodies are capable of. We know the nature and identity of our bodies by understanding their purpose, and purpose is never severed from the body's design. When we speak of male and female, we are speaking of those sexed persons whose bodily design bears a purpose toward a particular ultimate goal, namely, reproduction. Males and females are thus distinct beings, each with their own natures. That human beings have any fixed "nature" is what is at the core of the debate around transgender identities. The Christian worldview asserts that "nature" is central to our existence, while transgender voices insist that human nature is moldable. So underneath this debate is a debate we explored in the chapter on identity (chapter 6), and that is this: Are we to embrace our created nature, or are we free to alter our existence based on individual choice and will? Can we live against the truthfulness of our bodily design? No, we cannot. To do so is an active thwarting of what our bodies are designed to naturally do.

Sex difference is stable and unchanging. If maleness or femaleness is defined apart from the biological fact of our chromosomal makeup and the body's organization, male and female are pliable and meaningless terms open to endless interpretation and definition. The reason there are more "gender identities" than we have space to list, testifies to what happens when the fundamental markers of human identity are rejected: Something—anything—must fill the void. The most pernicious element of the transgender movement is the notion that one's "gender identity" is fluid. Despite the impression that "experts" agree with this new terminology, the notion of "gender identity" is a modern concept with no simple concrete definition. Furthermore, it cannot be empirically measured or verified.

Modern notions of "gender identity" define what it means to be male and female in ways that are foreign to the Bible—the "inner self," or a psychological state of mind. The theological and philosophical implication of the unchanging nature of man and woman is that a man cannot become a woman, and a woman cannot become a man. Sure, a doctor might surgically refashion certain body parts to look a certain way, but even then, the underlying reality of what gave us our male or female body—our chromosomes—cannot change. Surgery and cosmetology can only alter the exterior of the body, not its underlying nature.

The transgender worldview is built on incoherent foundations and internal contradictions. For one, there is no consensus on how to formulate what a "gender identity" even is. Is it innate? Is it socially constructed? Does it exist on a spectrum? These are proposals from transgender voices for determining what the concept means (leave aside the contradiction of something being "innate" while also "socially constructed"). We should also ask: How can modern feminism exist alongside transgenderism? Feminism implies a stable concept of womanhood for feminism to be real. Tensions exist even within the LGBTQ+ movement itself. Consider: How can homosexuality truly exist if maleness and femaleness are merely psychological categories? How can equality and fairness be meaningful concepts if males are allowed to compete against females? Both, obviously, are equal in worth, but their respective physical capacities are markers of sex differences that transgenderism denies should factor into competition. If "identity" is merely a measure of personal autonomy, what limiting principles are present to prevent absurd conclusions? As a friend of mine stated in a viral YouTube video: Why can't a short Caucasian American male identify as a tall Chinese woman?[1]

Compassion is owed to those who are psychologically vulnerable. Not everyone who reports having a conflict of gender identity is an activist bent on ideological domination. There are medically diagnosable conditions where individuals report a wrongfully perceived misalignment between their bodies and their minds. These individuals are owed compassion, mercy, and gentleness—not mockery, scorn, or contempt. It is Christianity's doctrine of human dignity that can defend the image bearer's inherent value while also insisting upon the essential truthfulness of a God-given, created nature.

The beauty of the Christian worldview surrounding questions of transgenderism is the sufficiency of the Christian worldview. Understanding the storyline of the Bible helps us make sense of transgenderism:

Creation → Fall → Redemption → Restoration

Understanding the storyline of Scripture allows us to understand God's original plan, why things are not as they should be, how the gospel empowers us to live lives of holiness in a broken creation, and where our ultimate hope lies.

Intersex conditions do not disprove the gender binary. Intersex conditions (of which there are many varieties) are often brought up in

1   Family Policy Institute of Washington, "Gender Identity: Can a 5'9, White Guy Be a 6'5, Chinese Woman?" (video), April 13, 2016, https://youtube.com.

conversations around transgenderism as a way of arguing that male and female exists on a spectrum. The argument is that intersex conditions disprove the stability of the gender binary. Though the issue is complex, a few things can be said in response:

(1) Intersex conditions are medically verifiable and diagnosable, whereas claims that someone is transgender are not.

(2) Intersex conditions are a recognition of a problem that exists against a typical medical standard. These conditions actually serve to reaffirm the abiding authority of the gender binary by recognizing a deviation from it.

(3) Despite ambiguities in anatomy, the majority of individuals who are intersex do not have confusion over whether they are male or female once chromosomes and other primary and secondary sex characteristics are discovered.

———

Here are some basic biblical, theological, and philosophical truths that every parent should know:

- The body's overall organization for reproduction is the most comprehensive way to account for male and female identity.
- Sex does not exist on a spectrum but is a binary.
- The transgender revolution requires individuals to believe falsehoods about human nature.
- If you abandon the biological basis of male and female, you must adopt absurd and contradictory claims to define what a man or woman is.

- Gender expression, while distinct from biological sex, cannot be severed from sex.
- We have a duty to love those reporting a perceived gender identity conflict.
- Intersex conditions are not a "third" sex nor do they prove that sex exists on a spectrum.

MEMORY VERSE

For I consider the sufferings of this present time are not worth comparing with the glory that is to be revealed to us. (Rom. 8:18)

THE FIRST FLOOR

Biblical Truths

- A *boy* is called a "male." A *girl* is called a "female."
- God created some of us males. God created some of us females (Gen. 1:26–28).
- Males and females are different in God's good plan.
- God created you for a purpose, and he has a plan for your life (Eph. 2:10).
- You cannot change who God created you to be.

Conversation Starters

- What is a boy called? What is a girl called?
- Whom did God create?
- Why are males and females different? What are some ways males and females are different?

- Why did God create you? What do you think God's plan for your life might be?
- Can you change how God created you? Why not?

THE SECOND FLOOR

Biblical Truths

- God made humanity in two forms: male and female (Gen. 1:26–28).
- God created males and females with different outward physical characteristics and different internal DNA.
- God created males and females differently on purpose. Our internal DNA triggers the reproductive differences and outward appearances that we associate with being male and female.
- God has a purpose and a plan for your life. You cannot change that purpose and plan by changing who you are on the outside. You will always be the same person God created you to be on the inside.
- Some people struggle with who God created them to be. Their bodies and minds get confused. But ultimately they are stuck in the fallenness of sin and need Jesus to save them. We should show them the love of Jesus and speak both grace and truth to them, not tease or mock them (Matt. 7:12).

Conversation Starters

- How many sexes are there? Can there be more? Why or why not?

- How did God create males and females the same and different? How do males and females look different on the outside? How are they different on the inside?
- Why did God create males and females different? Was that on purpose? Why? What happens if we mess with God's original design?
- Did God create you with a purpose and plan in mind? Can you change that? Can you be the opposite sex? If you change how you look on the outside, does that change the inside DNA of your body? Can you change your God-given, God-created biological sex?
- What is happening with some people who are confused about their bodies and want to be someone or something else? How can we love them and speak God's truth to them? Do you know anyone who is struggling with his or her body or mind? Have you ever struggled with your own body or mind? How can we (your parents) help you?

THE THIRD FLOOR

Biblical Truths

- God created two biological sexes: males and females. Gender is the social and cultural appropriateness through which we show the world our differences (Gen. 1:26–28).
- Gender expression is the way people show the world their masculinity and femininity through their appearance, mannerisms, and behavior. Gender expression cannot be separated from biological sex. For example, a male can

express himself as femininely as he wants, but he cannot be separated from his biological sex.

- God created males and females with distinct outward physical characteristics and internal XY or XX chromosomes. While outward physical characteristics can be changed, internal chromosomes will always remain male or female the way God created them.

- In God's creative brilliance, chromosomes determine each person's biological sex, which in turn gives shape to the physical differences in male and female bodies. While surgical interventions may try to alter our bodies, our chromosomes cannot change, and our sex remains exactly as God designed us. Trying to change maleness or femaleness is ultimately futile.

- God created male and female differences for the purpose of reproduction in marriage. Male and female bodies physically fit together like a puzzle. A male's sperm and a female's egg unite to create a new human being at the moment of conception.

- Sin has distorted how some people see their minds and their bodies. They are stuck in the fallenness of sin. Transgenderism is the belief that a person can change his or her outward body to become the opposite gender: male to female or female to male. Some people experience gender dysphoria (a conflict between their minds and their bodies) and will try to change their outward appearances, even with surgery or medicine, to try to bring peace to their restless minds and bodies. But this is just a falsehood about human nature and God's natural order of creation.

We have a duty to love those who express experiencing gender identity conflict. We should respond to them with the love of Jesus and speak in grace and truth, not mock and tease them (Matt. 7:12).

- The storyline of Scripture is creation → fall → redemption → restoration. Ultimately only Christ can fill the void of loneliness, acceptance, and love. The gospel gives us the power to live in the brokenness of a fallen creation while we wait for Christ's return to make all things new.

Conversation Starters

- How many biological sexes did God create? What is the difference between biological sex and gender? Can biological sex change? Can gender norms change?
- What's the difference between gender expression and biological sex? Can they be separated? How do people in our culture talk about this issue? What would your response be to the male who shaves, wears makeup and dresses, and talks in a high voice?
- What are the physical distinctions between males and females externally and internally? Can these be changed? Why or why not?
- Why did God create males and females different? What is reproduction? How do a male and female body work together to reproduce? Why should reproduction be saved for marriage of one man and one woman? Can you change your body outwardly? Can you change your body internally? What would you say about a man changing

his outward body to look like a woman's and saying that he was pregnant and wanted to nurse the baby?

• Do you believe that God has a plan and purpose for your life? Have you ever experienced feeling alone, unaccepted, or unloved? What did you do about those feelings? Did you ever feel that changing your outward body would help you feel better? How can we (your parents) help you?

• What is transgenderism? Do you know anyone who has a distorted view of his or her mind or body? Do you know anyone who has tried to change his or her body to become the opposite sex, transitioned with surgery or medicine, or who is transgendered? How would you respond to a friend who is struggling with feelings of gender dysphoria? Have you ever struggled with these types of feelings? How can we (your parents) help you or your friends? How are these distorted feelings of your mind and body falsehoods of human nature and God's natural order of creation? How can you speak to others struggling with transgenderism about the gospel of Jesus with grace and truth?

• How does the storyline of Scripture give you hope in the fallenness and sexual brokenness of this world? How does the gospel empower us to live in this fallen world of sexual brokenness? How do we love others and speak the truth while we wait for Christ's return? In what ways are our feelings not reliable guides? Can you recall a time where you felt a certain way only to later learn you were mistaken to feel the way you did? How can you test your feelings against Scripture? Why is following God's good and natural plan of creation the best way forward for you personally and, more generally, for our culture?

RECOMMENDED RESOURCES

Allberry, Sam. *What God Has to Say about Our Bodies: How the Gospel Is Good News for Our Physical Selves.* Wheaton, IL: Crossway, 2021.

Anderson, Ryan T. *When Harry Became Sally.* San Francisco: Ignatius Press, 2019.

Branch, J. Alan. *Affirming God's Image: Addressing the Transgender Question with Science and Scripture.* Bellingham, WA: Lexham Press, 2019.

James, Sharon. *Gender Ideology: What Do Christians Need to Know?* Fearn, UK: Christian Focus, 2019.

Walker, Andrew T. *God and the Transgender Debate.* 2nd edition. Charlotte, NC: The Good Book Company, 2022.

8

Technology

IN THE NOT-TOO-RECENT PAST, news outlets reported that large social media companies had a trove of research looking at how their platforms were affecting the mental health of their users. The results were staggering. Usage correlated with increased depression and anxiety. These algorithmically curated experiences were engineered for the sake of exploiting human weakness.

This all came home for me when I (Andrew) had to stop reading the daily news on my iPad during the early days of the COVID-19 pandemic because it was affecting my attitude. I would doomscroll through the news and notice my state of mind affected, which in turn shaped how the day would unfold.

Companies have learned to benefit their bottom line by manipulating people's emotions. For example, the pornography crisis deadens society to the sanctity of marital intercourse. Our digital ecosystem lets politically correct sex trafficking—pornography— prey on our instincts. This is to say nothing of the ongoing debates about how political regimes or private companies can harvest data in order to influence elections.

The rage of toxic polarization has been weaponized by the anonymity of keyboards. And then there is the next frontier: Artificial Intelligence (AI), a breathtaking technology with yet-to-be-discovered possibilities.

It goes without saying that technology, particularly all of life in the digital age, is presenting us with a dizzying array of possibilities when it comes to where we spend our time, how we understand who we are, and how we perceive the world around us. No stone is left unturned when it comes to technology. Technology is not just a "thing" we use; it colors virtually every interaction we have in the world today. We use technology but then technology shapes us into the types of persons that further technology's demands. It's an unending cycle of compulsion-desire-formation.

The most important lesson we want to draw out in this chapter is simple: carelessness toward technology will see you and your household swept up in its power. If there's any call to action that we want to convey in this chapter, it is the importance of active engagement with your child's (and family's) technology use.

BIBLICAL TEACHING OVERVIEW

Technology is an instrument of common grace. Technology is present in every part of the Bible's creation, fall, redemption, and restoration storyline. When God placed Adam and Eve in the garden, their responsibility was to cultivate and develop it for the sake of productivity. God, in essence, gives us the raw materials and tells us to shape and mold them toward culturally beneficial ends. Harnessing the raw materials of this world and channeling them into productive use captures the heart of exercising dominion over creation (Gen. 1:26–28). After the fall, technological development continued to proceed (Gen. 4:20–22), though technology could also now be harnessed in idolatrous ways (Gen. 11:1–9). Redemption offers the ability for technology to be used in God-glorifying ways. The new creation is described as a city where kings bring their glory (Rev. 21:24), which would have to include the elements of culture developed through technological advances. Rather than adopting a separatist mindset that views technology as inherently corrupting, the Bible views technology as the outgrowth of human creativity that can be used for both good and sinful purposes.

Technology, on its own, is about how it is used, not only whether it is used. Ever since the invention of the wheel, technology has afforded its users the ability to streamline, simplify, and create. What this means is that the moral worth of any technological instrument is determined by how it is used. A computer, for example, can be used to create and distribute pornography. The same model computer, used by someone else, can be used to write books to help Christian parents (like the computer we're using to write this book). Christian wisdom about technology must take into consideration what we're using our technology *for*. If you're an adult who insists on technology's presence throughout every area of your life, have you considered whether it is an impediment too? If you're a parent, would you rather engage your child's

attention or have a tablet do so? These are all probing questions that require us to examine our hearts. The principles of wisdom that govern the Christian's life on any number of topics should also guide our principles when it comes to technology. Consider Philippians 4:8: "Finally, brothers, whatever is true, whatever is honorable, whatever is just, whatever is pure, whatever is lovely, whatever is commendable, if there is any excellence, if there is anything worthy of praise, think about these things." Our use of any technological device should be funneled through the grid of whether the item in question is training us for righteousness or unrighteousness.

We are affective beings, not just rational beings. "What you put in, you get out." You may have heard your parent or youth pastor repeat this saying when you were a kid. It's a riff off a more biblical truth found in Matthew 12:34–35: "For out of the abundance of the heart the mouth speaks. The good person out of his good treasure brings forth good, and the evil person out of his evil treasure brings forth evil." While humans are thinking beings, we are also deeply feeling beings, too. Our emotions and our desires can be shaped consciously or unconsciously by what we ingest, consume, or familiarize ourselves with over time. Consider your phone. How many of us rationally evaluate our decision to pick up our phones and scroll versus just picking up our phones out of automated muscle memory? How many of us can scroll through Twitter or watch an Instagram reel and look up and not notice that forty minutes went by? We must be deeply, deeply discerning, intentional, and discriminating of the media and technology we consume. If we aren't intentional, we will not only be consuming technology uncritically, we'll be consumed ourselves by the forces vying for our attention, our affections, and, ultimately, our souls. I'm sure you, like us, have seen someone's use of technology destroy his or her life, whether with pornography or narcissistic behavior on social media. No one starts out thinking that's where he or she is headed, but the ways we can passively consume technology and media can be incredibly deforming to us behaviorally and spiritually.

Technology cannot replace reality. "Touch grass" is one of our favorite online phrases. The term is used, sarcastically, to basically say to someone, "You need to get off the internet and remember what real life is like." It's a phrase directed at the chronically-online person whose life is too consumed by online skirmishes. While there may not be one Bible verse that captures the sentiment of what we're urging here, consider the very presentation of creation order and reality that Scripture presents us with: All of us are enfleshed persons meant to live alongside one another in our embodiment and not merely in a disembodied state where all our interactions are online. The offer of endless online euphoria robs us of the deeper connections we are meant to experience in the bodies God has given us. Digital community cannot replace real-life community. Not only can digital community not replace real-life community, but digital community is also a cheap substitute for the real-life riches that God means for us.

———

Here are some basic biblical, theological, and philosophical principles that every Christian parent should know:

- Technology's value is measured by whether it is pointing us to God and his word or away from it.
- Technology can be used for good and for bad.
- Technology should be seen as a gift to build civilization and provide better controls around safeguarding life.
- Technology cannot remove humanity's greatest problem: sin. No amount of technology will be adequate as the all-sufficient balm that we often view it to be.
- Intentionality is pivotal in thinking through the unintended consequences of technological influence.
- Christians should adopt neither an instinctual rejection nor an instinctual acceptance of technology. All parents must examine, study, and plan for how their children will use technology.
- A child's interaction with technology should not be with an "off-on" switch but a dimmer switch. Children need to slowly adjust to the technology available to them, not simply be thrown into the deep end to fend for themselves.
- A source of Christian witness in the society we live in today is to prevent our Christian homes from falling prey to the temptation to isolate ourselves in order to let technology entertain us individually (often in separate rooms or on separate devices). The family itself must confront technology by how technology is impacting the family itself, not just individuals.

MEMORY VERSE

Finally, brothers, whatever is true, whatever is honorable, whatever is just, whatever is pure, whatever is lovely, whatever is commendable, if there is any excellence, if there is anything worthy of praise, think about these things. (Phil. 4:8)

THE FIRST FLOOR

Biblical Truths

- God gives humans the creative ability to build and create things, like technology (TV, iPads, tablets, phones, screens, etc.) (Gen. 4:17–22).
- Technology can be good and help us learn.
- Too much technology is not good for us.
- God gives dads and moms the authority to tell when you (the child) can use technology (Ex. 20:12).
- God tells boys and girls to obey dads and moms because their job is to keep their children safe and healthy (Eph. 6:1–3).

Conversation Starters

- What did God give humans the ability to do? What kinds of things do you like to build and create? What kinds of things are part of technology? Do you like playing with technology?
- Can technology be good? What can technology help us do? How does your technology help you learn?
- Is too much technology good or bad for us? Why is it bad?

- Who gives Dad and Mom authority over you? What is authority? Who gets to decide how much technology you get to use?
- When Dad and Mom tell you it's time to turn off your technology, do you obey? What is their job? Are they keeping you safe and healthy when they turn off your technology?

THE SECOND FLOOR

Biblical Truths

- God gives the ability to shape and mold raw materials into something productive, like technology (Gen. 4:17–22).
- Technology can be good if it brings glory and honor to God. Technology can be bad if it is corrupted by sin (1 Cor. 10:31).
- Technology must be limited for your good.
- God has given authority to your parents to plan how you will use technology, where you will use technology, and to put limits on your technology (Eph. 6:1–3).
- God has called you to obey your parents in all things. Your parents' job is to keep you safe and healthy. They are trying to protect your development while you use technology (Ex. 20:12).

Conversation Starters

- What does God give humans the ability to create? What has our God-given creativity led humans to create?

- Is technology good? Is technology bad? What falls under the term "technology?"
- Why should technology be limited? Why is that for your good?
- What authority has God given your parents? How do they use that authority?
- What has God called you to do? What is your parents' job? How do they keep you safe and healthy? How does this protect you when you are using technology? How does this protect you when they limit your technology? Are you obeying them with technology?

THE THIRD FLOOR

Biblical Truths

- God gives humans dominion over his creation. Humans taking raw materials and channeling them into productive use is at the very heart of exercising dominion over creation. Technology grows out of human creativity (Gen. 4:17–22).
- Technology should be treated like any other invention: Is this training me for righteousness or unrighteousness? The same principles that guide the Christian life are the same principles that should be guiding the use of technology. Technology can be good if used to help us learn and train in righteousness. Technology can be bad if used for sin (Phil. 4:8).
- Technology affects our thoughts, emotions, and desires. It must be safeguarded, protected, and limited. Our hearts

are filling up through what we hear and see. When we consume, ingest, and familiarize ourselves with media over time, our affections will be pulled to Christ or away from him. We must be intentional and critical about what we consume. We must protect and limit how much time we spend on our devices and what we are doing on our devices (Matt. 12:34–35).

- Digital connections and community cannot replace real-life connections and community. Online friendships and relationships do not provide true intimacy or physical connectedness. God desires us to be in community with other believers and enjoy the rich blessings of this life (Prov. 27:17).

- God has provided parents to safeguard your heart, mind, and development through limiting your technology. God has given your parents authority over you, and you are called to obey their authority (Eph. 6:1–3).

Conversation Starters

- How do humans show dominion over God's creation? How is technology a productive use of human creativity?

- Is technology good or bad? Have you ever asked yourself if technology is training you for righteousness or unrighteousness? Do you have righteous technology? Do you have unrighteous technology? Is there some technology that you need to get rid of? Do you need help?

- Why does technology need to be safe-guarded, protected, and limited? Have you lived with limited or unlimited technology? How has that impacted you? How have your affections (thoughts, emotions, desires) been formed through what you have consumed? Do you need to rethink what you are consuming? Are there things that are pulling you away from Christ? How can we (your parents) help you?

- Do you have more digital community or real-life community? What differences are there between online friendships and real-life friendships? How can you be in community with other believers and enjoy God's blessings in this life?
- What are your parents trying to do when they limit your technology? Who has given your parents authority over you? What is authority? How are you called to respond to their authority? How are you called to respond if you do not agree with their decisions? Have you disagreed with your parents in this area? How have you responded? How should you realign your heart with an understanding of God's plan?

RECOMMENDED RESOURCES

Crouch, Andy. *The Tech-Wise Family*. Grand Rapids, MI: Baker Books, 2017.

James, Samuel. *Digital Liturgies: Rediscovering Christian Wisdom in an Online Age*. Wheaton, IL: Crossway, 2023.

Reinke, Tony. *12 Ways Your Phone Is Changing You*. Wheaton, IL: Crossway, 2017.

Thacker, Jason. *Following Jesus in a Digital Age*. Nashville, TN: B&H Publishing, 2022.

9

Political Engagement

WHEN I (ANDREW) speak at a church or conference, I never fail
to get a question from an exhausted and frustrated person who
throws up his hands in despair at the condition of American
culture and asks, "What can be done?"

I've memorized my response:

We can each do something. I, personally, can teach and write
about how Christians should care about these issues. The issue
is not that Christians do not have answers to today's greatest
challenges; it is that, at the end of the day, political change
is about amassing a sufficient number of people who share
a common goal. It requires organizing and mobilizing; and
unless we can persuade others of the correctness of what we
believe, venting frustrations won't tangibly change anything.
Changing your world doesn't happen by complaining but by
slow plodding and persuasion.

This means . . . politics. The same Christians who are upset at the corrosive effects of Western culture are the same Christians who often do not know the name of their local state representative or chafe at the idea of running for school board because that would take time.

Now, we should also be clear about something: as important as political engagement is, no earthly political utopia is possible. Politics on this side of heaven often amounts to mitigating the effects of sin more than it does to ensuring the perfect political community. But realistic expectations about what's possible in a fallen age with lots of different people living in a community do not lessen the importance of being aware of what is going on in your community and fighting joyfully and doggedly for justice. Some may disagree with what we're about to say, but we think being a faithful Christian means faithful stewardship and faithful attentiveness to where one lives and what is happening that affects the lives of everyone. You have an obligation to know what is happening in your world and your community and to work in the ways appropriate to you, to see justice and righteousness reign (Jer. 29:4–7). We do not see this as the mission of the church, but the mission of godly citizens to shape their cities, states, and nation for the good.

If you're a Christian parent, we're not saying that you need to be listening to talk radio, watching cable news, or doomscrolling on social media all day long for the most fevered political views that are out there, but you should not have your head buried in the sand either. There is as much caution necessary to protect yourself from being politically obsessive as there is the need to reject political apathy. Apathy and obsession are equally alike in being the wrong approach to political engagement.

BIBLICAL TEACHING OVERVIEW

Government is a divine institution authorized by God. The goal of any earthly political regime is to recognize the inherent rights of human beings that are made in God's image, promote systems of equal justice under systems of law, facilitate access to the common good, and punish evil deeds that human beings commit against one another (Gen. 9:5–6; Rom. 13:1–7; 1 Pet. 2:13–17). Christians are to be scripturally faithful citizens who view the state as a legitimate arm of God's authority on earth to serve society's welfare. Christians should respect, obey, and honor the state and comply with its laws insofar as they do not command disobedience to God (Acts 5:29). The government's role is limited to areas that concern earthly affairs only. The government is not designed to referee or resolve theological debates or to point you to a saving relationship with Christ. Similarly, unjust political rulers and political systems are condemned in Scripture for ruthless and unjust conduct (Dan. 3; Matt. 2:16–18). Even if government is not meant to interfere or involve itself directly in religious matters, government and rulers are still accountable to God's standards for civil justice (Prov. 8:14–16).

Christians are to be good citizens. Christians are called to honor their authorities, obey laws, and live justly. Citizenship in an earthly political community should not subvert, conflict, or be confused with one's primary heavenly citizenship. Though not a contradiction to one another, your membership in God's kingdom requires a higher allegiance than membership in an earthly kingdom. Christians are to seek the welfare of their communities (1 Tim. 2:1–4; 1 Pet. 2:13–17). Remembering that Christ is supreme, Christians should participate in politics with an eye toward wisdom, justice, and righteousness for the sake of the common good. We should understand that politics is one arena that allows us to order our societies for our good and God's glory.

Ensuring the common good is the purpose of politics. The common good is the set of conditions in society allowing individuals, groups, and institutions to flourish respectively to their purpose. Government setting up policies that allow families to prosper, for example, is how the common good is achieved. The common good promotes justice for all. For this purpose, political engagement is going to look very ordinary as we strive for conditions that allow human beings to live, families to thrive, and communities to prosper. Politics is little else than how to organize our lives together.

It is appropriate and good to allow one's religious convictions to shape one's political convictions. Not all theological convictions translate neatly to matters of politics. For example, the state should not have a position on whether Baptists or Presbyterians are correct about baptism. But the state cannot be indifferent, for example, on whether unborn children have the right to life. (They do!) While that is, on the one hand, a theological claim issuing from Genesis, it is a philosophical claim, as well. It is a statement that one must agree or disagree with regardless of whether one accepts the presuppositions of our faith. It is fine for religious convictions to shape your politics (and they absolutely should!), but it is also the responsibility of people with a religiously grounded claim to explain why their view on any given subject matters for everyone in society. Not everybody has an interest in questions of baptism in the same way that everyone has an interest in whether life can be terminated in the womb.

Political engagement is a worthwhile pursuit. Though fallen, politics is a legitimate sphere of God's providence. The presence of Christians helps political orders understand and attain their fullest possible horizons for justice, human flourishing, and the common good. Just because politics is about "power" does not mean that a Christian exercising political power is compromising or worldly. All politics rely upon power. Power itself is morally neutral; the question is the *end* to which political power is wielded, which is either in the direction of moral goodness and justice or away from them. An account of the legitimate use of power for the sake of justice and the common good is essential to the task of statecraft.

The message of the New Testament is not a directly political message because God's kingdom is not synonymous with or reducible to earthly political kingdoms. Christianity does not call for the overthrow of earthly political regimes. But as Christianity grew throughout history, it did take on political significance as Christians came to dominate society and shape laws after Christian values. There is nothing inherently wrong with that happening. Politics is messy, meaning there are examples of Christianity getting corrupted by the worldliness of politics, but also examples of Christians doing heroic things through politics in order to combat a moral evil.

Political engagement is a forum for loving one's neighbor by seeking your neighbor's flourishing. Christians have a responsibility to ensure that laws reflect the righteousness of God's standards for his creation. Christians should not engage in politics for the sake of their own interests but in the interest of what causes all people to have the best chance to prosper. Forfeiting responsibility to one's neighbor by allowing their exposure to evil is not to act in Christian love. We would do well to remember Jeremiah's instructions where exiled Israel is instructed to "seek the welfare of the city where I have sent you into exile, and pray to the LORD on its behalf, for in its welfare you will find your welfare" (Jer. 29:7).

The solution to political apathy is not political idolatry. For some people, they care too much about politics (that's often the case for me, Andrew). Others care too little about politics (that's regularly the case for Christian). It's important to establish a healthy equilibrium.

Christians must practice important virtues when it comes to political engagement. Because politics often concerns very detailed policy questions, there will always be some level of disagreement as to what is best for a given society. Prudence is thus very necessary for determining what policies work best. There will be policies where Christians disagree (e.g., gun control and healthcare). At the same time, there are pressing moral realities that Christians cannot disagree on (e.g., the right to life, the identity of male and female, and the definition of marriage). Christians must exercise great discernment in learning what various parties and platforms stand for and to what degree Christians are giving material support to parties, platforms, and politicians that support unambiguous moral evil. We must understand that ethical obedience is tied to the gospel. No matter how much prudence is involved, it is not consistent for Christians to vote for parties, platforms, or candidates who will knowingly perpetuate an intrinsic evil.

Christians must not be hyperpartisan and must be willing to practice intellectual honesty and consistency whenever their favorite politicians or political parties err. We must judge all platforms, parties, and politicians impartially, giving favor to none over others because of a personal allegiance or preference. Christians would do well to expose themselves to a variety of media outlets in order to prevent themselves from getting cocooned in a political echo chamber. Lastly, Christians must practice civility and agreeableness (Col. 4:5–6; 1 Pet. 3:15–17). We must be *both* courageous and civil. If the Bible forges no division between the two, neither should we.

———

Here are some basic biblical, theological, and philosophical principles that every Christian parent should know:

- Christian participation in the public square requires pursuing justice, social responsibilities, and a concern for human rights.
- Christians should be attentive to how political discussions impact public justice, the natural family, religious liberty, and public morality. The creation order categories of *existence*, *identity*, and *family* are three domains to be attentive to when it comes to the impact of politics on all three.
- Politics is coordinated action for the sake of justice.

- Elections have real-life consequences that affect society for good and for ill.
- The best way to engage politically is by starting at the local level.
- Christians should treat government officials with respect even if they strongly disagree with them.
- In political debate, it is important to identify where the disagreement lies. Identifying where disagreement is really helps chart a path for mutual understanding of divergent perspectives.
- Avoiding personal insults in political conversation is very important to maintain a spirit of civility.
- While lamentable, polarization is inevitable as worldview differences grow more stark between competing political parties, platforms, and candidates.
- There is no inherent virtue or vice in being in the political minority or the political majority. What matters is the moral content of what one's politics are.
- Romanticizing political persecution is tone-deaf and fails to account for how real-life involvement in law-making can affect politics and culture in positive ways.
- As Carl F. H. Henry once remarked, it is the responsibility of the church to "declare the criteria by which nations will ultimately be judged, and the divine standards to which man and society must conform if civilization is to endure."[1]

---

1   Carl F. H. Henry, "An Ecumenical Bombshell," *Christianity Today*, September 15, 1967, 28.

MEMORY VERSE

But seek the welfare of the city where I have sent you into exile, and pray to the LORD on its behalf, for in its welfare you will find your welfare. (Jer. 29:7)

THE FIRST FLOOR

Biblical Truths

- The government is the institution in charge of making laws for the country or state. It makes rules and laws to protect its citizens (people) who live in the country and state. Those rules and laws keep the citizens safe and punish the citizens who make bad choices (Rom. 13:1–7).
- All government is under God's authority. God is in charge of everything in heaven and on earth.
- The government makes rules to help protect families and children and help the community (all the people who live and work together in one city or region).
- We should care about our government because Jesus tells us to love one another. We should help our government as it helps our neighbors and community live well together (Jer. 29:4–7).
- God tells us to obey our earthly leaders when they make laws about how we live on earth (1 Pet. 2:13–17).
- We must be kind and loving even when we disagree with others (Col. 4:6).

Conversation Starters

- Who is in charge of the country? Who makes rules and laws? What do rules and laws do?
- Government is under whose authority? God is in charge of what?
- What kind of rules does the government make? Are these rules good or bad?
- Should we care about the government? Why should we care about the government? Why should we care about our neighbors? How do you care about your neighbors?
- Whom does God tell us to obey? When do we obey our earthly leaders?
- Will we always agree with everyone? How should we act if we disagree with someone? Have you ever disagreed with someone before? How did you act?

THE SECOND FLOOR

Biblical Truths

- Government makes rules and laws to protect citizens of countries and states. The goal of the government is to recognize the God-given rights of human beings, keep citizens safe, and punish evil (Rom. 13:1–7).
- Government is under God's authority and is designed for the common good of family and community.
- The common good is when government makes laws in a way that allows human beings to live, families to grow, and communities to develop.

- God calls us to love our neighbor. Loving your neighbor will lead you to be involved in government and desire laws that allow their lives to flourish (Jer. 29:4–7).
- God calls us to obey our earthly leaders. We are to obey, respect, and honor the government, as long as it doesn't disobey God's commands (1 Pet. 2:13–17).
- We must speak with truth and grace when we disagree about politics (Col. 4:6).

Conversation Starters

- What is the job of the government? Do you think that the government always meets its goals correctly? Why or why not?
- Whose authority is the government under? How was the government designed? Who designed it that way? Why do you think God designed the government for us on earth?
- What is the common good? What kind of laws do you know about that allow human beings to live, families to grow, and communities to develop?
- How are you expected to interact with your neighbor? How do you show love to your neighbor? If you love your neighbor, how will that lead you to want to be involved in government and law-making that is good for them? What are some laws that are good for your neighbor?
- How are you expected to interact with your earthly leaders? Do you obey, respect, and honor the government and its leaders? When would you not obey the government?
- What does it mean to speak with truth and grace about politics? Have you ever disagreed with someone about

politics? How did you respond in that disagreement? How could you have a disagreement and speak in truth and grace?

THE THIRD FLOOR
Biblical Truths

- The goal of any earthly political regime is to recognize the inherent rights of human beings, promote systems of equal justice under the law, facilitate access to the common good, and punish evil deeds that human beings commit against one another (Rom. 13:1–7).
- The common good is the benefit or interest of all people in a group or society. As Christians, we should engage in politics to pursue the common good that allows individuals, groups, and institutions to flourish for their purpose: human beings to live, families to thrive, and communities to prosper. Politics is how we organize our lives together (Jer. 29:4–7).
- Prudence is the virtue of exercising attentiveness or caution to possible danger. Christians must be prudent when it comes to political policies. We will not all agree on what policies are best. Some policies can be held lightly and debated among Christians: gun control and healthcare. Other policies are moral realities that must be held tightly among Christians: for example, the right to life, the identity of male and female, and the definition of marriage. We must be discerning about what parties, platforms, and

politicians we are willing to support who will knowingly stand for or against moral evil (Ps. 34:14).

- God calls Christians to obey, respect, and honor the state and comply with its laws up to the point of disobedience to God's commands. The government is not designed to point you to God or solve theological debates. Government's role is limited to earthly issues.
- Christians must be courageous and civil. We will disagree about policies, politicians, platforms, etc. Avoiding personal insults in political conversation is very important to maintain decorum. We must practice civility and learn how to agree well and also how to disagree amicably (Col. 4:6).
- The best place to engage with the government is at the local level. And don't forget to register to vote when you turn eighteen.

Conversation Starters

- How should Christians see government authorities and laws? How far should Christians take obedience to earthly government? Why is the government limited?
- Will we always agree on politics? What should happen when we disagree? Have you ever had a disagreement regarding politics or policies? How did you handle that conversation? How could you handle it differently next time?
- What is the goal of the government for how God intended it? What are human rights? How do we recognize the inherent rights of human beings and whether our

laws reflect God's standard for justice? How do we promote equality of justice under the law and what needs to
change to better reflect God's standard of justice? How
do we promote the common good? How do we punish
evil deeds? Looking at the many forms of government
in the world, who is doing this well and who is doing
this poorly? Why? What do you think is the best form
of government and why? What do you think is the worst
form of government and why?

- What is the common good, and why, as Christians, should
we pursue it? How do you see the government allowing
human beings to live, families to thrive, and communities to prosper? Do you agree that politics can be boiled
down as simply as organizing our lives together? Why or
why not?

- What is prudence, and why is this a virtue Christians must
exercise in the political arena? What does it mean that
some policies can be held loosely and some policies must
be held tightly? What policies do you think Christians
must agree on, and what policies do you think Christians
can disagree on? What is moral evil? Why must we be so
diligent and discerning when it comes to political platforms, politicians, parties, etc., when it comes to moral
evil? Have you ever liked a politician but disagreed with
his or her policy? How did you think through that issue?

- How should Christians respond to government authority?
What is the government's role between earthly affairs and
heavenly affairs? How far should we take our commitment
to politics and the government?

- Have you ever disagreed with someone about politics or policies? How did you handle that? What does God say about how we should handle disagreement as Christians? Can we allow politics to create division within our church or among Christian brothers and sisters? How can you plan to debate these heated topics next time?
- Where is the best place to get involved? When can you register to vote?

RECOMMENDED RESOURCES

Beckwith, Francis. *Politics for Christians: Statecraft as Soulcraft.* Downers Grove, IL: IVP Academic, 2010.

Innes, David C. *Christ and the Kingdoms of Men: Foundations of Political Life.* Phillipsburg, NJ: P&R, 2019.

Leeman, Jonathan. *How the Nations Rage.* Nashville, TN: Nelson, 2018.

VanDrunen, David. *Politics after Christendom: Political Theology in a Fractured World.* Grand Rapids, MI: Zondervan Academic, 2020.

Walker, Andrew T. *Faithful Reason: Natural Law Ethics for God's Glory and Our Good.* Nashville, TN: B&H Academic, 2024.

Walker, Andrew T. *Liberty for All: Defending Everyone's Religious Freedom in a Secular Age.* Grand Rapids, MI: Brazos Press, 2021.

Walker, Andrew T. *The Nations Belong to God: A Christian Guide for Political Engagement.* Ethics and Religious Liberty Commission, 2024.

10

Hostility and Persecution

IF YOU ARE READING THIS BOOK, you are likely the parent of a child growing up in a culture that neither you nor we grew up in. A span of fifteen years, roughly 2000–2015, marked a rapid change in American culture. Changes previously considered radical are now routine. Same-sex marriage and preferred pronouns now seem as American as baseball and apple pie. To be clear, the changes that took place were set in motion decades ago, but the culmination of those previous shifts reached their zenith between 2000–2015. In those years, radical changes around identity, sexuality, and gender supplanted older ways of seeing the world, ways that primarily, reflected the influence of Christianity.

What that means for you (and us) as parents is that to be Christian and to raise young Christians in this culture requires a fortitude that previous generations did not have to cultivate to the same degree. Preparing our children to withstand the tsunami of culture means preparing them to enter a world where their Christian faith is viewed as eccentric or bigoted. To put it as simply as we can: there is now a social cost to being a Christian in many of America's most elite sectors. But there is also good news: statistics show that a child who grows up in a home where family discipleship takes place and where church activities are put first makes him or her dramatically less likely to abandon the faith once he or she leaves the nest. But those things must begin *now*—especially to survive in a climate where abandoning your Christian upbringing is edgy and supposedly "freeing."

Now, there are a few ways to think about hostility and persecution. There is a false way to glamorize persecution as though it's a mark of authentic Christianity, as though smallness and marginalization are virtues in themselves. This, I believe, is naive. I (Andrew) teach students from cultures where the government persecutes the Christian faith, and if you ask these students, all of them would love to have the religious liberty that American Christians enjoy. Then there is the tendency that some have to view any disagreement or criticism as outright persecution. While persecution exists in shades and degrees, being quick on the draw to label everything "persecution" can often ring very hollow. A better way, we think, to view persecution is that it is an occasion to soberly identify with our Lord and Savior, Jesus Christ, who experienced the very worst fate of persecution and hostility: martyrdom. But he was also insulted, mocked, and challenged by fierce opposition by very powerful people. Refinement in times of difficulty and challenge means there is renewed opportunity for Christians to deepen their faith and to re-articulate the faith "once for all delivered" through diligent study, like-minded fellowship, and the practice of Christian hope (Jude 3).

Regardless, a shifting culture requires Christians to adapt themselves to stand firm and minister wisely in our culture.

BIBLICAL TEACHING OVERVIEW

Christians are called to be immovable in their faith. Christian doctrine is not something from which a person can pick and choose what to believe and obey. Orthodoxy (doctrine) and orthopraxy (ethics) are a package deal. We cannot selectively decide what we want to believe or obey without damaging the internal integrity and consistency of Christian doctrine. Our call as Christians is to "guard the deposit" of faith entrusted to us (1 Tim. 6:20; 2 Tim. 1:14). Whether we call it stubbornness or bullheadedness, Christians must develop a posture of resolve and humble courage. Of course, this must be done with gentleness and respect and with a concern not to harm our witness (Col. 4:5–6; 1 Pet. 3:15). But we do not calibrate what we believe based on whether it is popular with the world.

Persecution follows after the example of Jesus. Christians should never consider themselves beyond receiving what Jesus himself went through and promised his followers they would also go through. As Jesus teaches in John 15:18–21:

> If the world hates you, know that it has hated me before it hated you. If you were of the world, the world would love you as its own; but because you are not of the world, but I chose you out of the world, therefore the world hates you. Remember the word that I said to you: "A servant is not greater than his master." If they persecuted me, they will also persecute you. If they kept my word, they will also keep yours. But all these things they will do to you on account of my name, because they do not know him who sent me.

The apostle Paul also predicted in 2 Timothy 3:12 that "all who desire to live a godly life in Christ Jesus will be persecuted."

In the history of the Christian church, some degree of persecution has been present literally everywhere. The hardships that many Western Christians face now are hardships that non-Western Christians face regularly.

Persecution provides a unique communion with Jesus. As unexpected as it may sound, Jesus considers persecution for his sake to be a source of spiritual blessing. In other words, we reap a spiritual benefit when criticized or harassed for following Christ. As Jesus says in Matthew 5:10–12:

> Blessed are those who are persecuted for righteousness' sake, for theirs is the kingdom of heaven. Blessed are you when others revile you and persecute you and utter all kinds of evil against you falsely on my account. Rejoice and be glad, for your reward is great in heaven, for so they persecuted the prophets who were before you.

The formula isn't necessarily logical according to the world's standards. Still, when Christians face trials for their faith, Scripture promises that their relationships with Christ are strengthened— even to the point of increased joy as was true of the apostles, who counted it as joy to suffer for Christ's sake (Acts 5:41). Facing genuine hostility or persecution and our response to it may be the test that determines whether one's commitment to Christ is superficial or deeply rooted (Matt. 13:1–23).

We must rely on Jesus when faced with persecution. Jesus tells us to "not be anxious" while looking to God for our provision (Matt. 6:25–34). We must trust the fatherly benevolence of the Lord to care for and minister to us when encountering hostility. Moreover, Scripture admonishes us to trust in Jesus during the actual moment of persecution and hatred, for his Spirit will guide us in times of trial (Luke 12:11–12).

Our ultimate goal and hope is not in cultural or worldly conquest but in Jesus's final victory. While Christians should be present in the world, contending for the truth of Scripture in every arena where God has placed us, we cannot ensure that cultural victory is ours in this age. Even still, we are called to witness to the truth for the sake of truth itself, not because it will be met with total gladness or joy by all, but because the proclamation of the gospel is the means by which the Lord redeems those he's called to salvation. It is important to put the words of John 16:33 in our hearts: "I have said these things to you, that in me you may have peace. In the world you will have tribulation. But take heart; I have overcome the world."

Here are some biblical, theological, and philosophical truths that every Christian parent should know:

- The biblical formula for experiencing persecution includes understanding there will be spiritual benefit from it.
- It is through times of trial and testing that Christian faith matures.

- We should not invite hostility or persecution but embrace it as a necessary reality flowing out of our conviction that God's word is inerrant, authoritative, and sufficient.
- If Christians are to thrive amid growing cultural opposition, they must commit to a deeper understanding of their faith.
- We are called to be truthful and gracious in our communication with nonbelievers, but kindness and winsomeness are not guarantees that we will not experience persecution.
- The importance of Christian friendship is invaluable in enduring hardship, hostility, testing, or persecution. A community of friends, particularly in your local church, who will have your back, pray for you, and affirm your faith is essential for Christian discipleship.

MEMORY VERSE

Therefore, my beloved brothers, be steadfast, immovable, always abounding in the work of the Lord, knowing that in the Lord your labor is not in vain. (1 Cor. 15:58)

THE FIRST FLOOR
Biblical Truths

- Christians believe that God's word is true, tells us what to do, and has everything we need to know (2 Tim. 3:16–17).
- Christians have faith in Jesus. Faith is trusting and believing in Jesus even though we cannot see him (Heb. 11:1).

- Some people don't like Jesus. Some people won't like us because we follow Jesus (John 15:20).
- Jesus says he will be with us and make our faith deeper when people don't like us (John 15:18–21).
- Christians need church and Christian friends to help them grow in their faith (James 5:16).
- When things in this world are hard, remember that Jesus has overcome the world (John 16:33)!

Conversation Starters

- What do we believe about God's word? What does it mean that God's word is true? What does God's word tell us to do? What does it mean that God's word tells us everything we need to know? What are some things that you know God's word says?
- What is faith? Whom do we have faith in? Can we see Jesus? Do we still believe Jesus is alive even though we can't see him? Where is Jesus?
- Does everyone in the world like Jesus? Will everyone like us? Why not?
- Since some people won't like us, who will still be with us? How will Jesus help our faith? How do you feel Jesus is with you?
- Do we need church? Do we need friends? How do our friends help us grow our faith? How can you be a good friend to others?
- Have things ever been hard for you? What does it mean that Jesus has overcome the world?

THE SECOND FLOOR

Biblical Truths

- As Christians, we believe that God's word is *inerrant* (meaning it has zero errors), is the ultimate authority, and is *sufficient* (meaning it is enough for us, and it needs nothing added or taken away) (2 Tim. 3:16–17).
- As Christians, our faith is in Jesus. We do not get to pick what we believe or obey based upon how the world around us changes. We believe and obey Jesus because he never changes.
- Jesus tells us that we will face persecution (hostility and ill-treatment) because we follow him. The world hates Jesus and therefore hates his followers (John 15:18).
- Jesus says that we should count it a blessing to be persecuted as he was persecuted: "Rejoice and be glad, for your reward is great in heaven" (Matt. 5:10–12). Our faith will be strengthened in times of trial.
- Christians need a local church community and Christian friendships to provide prayer and encouragement as we grow in faith (James 5:16).
- When people don't like us and persecution feels difficult, remember that Jesus has already overcome the world (John 16:33)!

Conversation Starters

- What do we believe about God's word? What does *inerrant* mean? What does *ultimate authority* mean? What does *sufficient* mean? What are some things that you know about God's word?

- What is *faith*? Whom do we put our faith in? What would happen if we just kept changing what we believed or obeyed as the world changed around us? Why do we believe and obey Jesus? How do you feel knowing that he never changes? Why is it better to believe in Jesus (who is never changing) than in the world (that is always changing)?

- What is *persecution*? What does Jesus tell us about persecution? Why will we face persecution? What do we do that makes us face persecution? Have you ever faced any kind of hostility or ill-treatment because you follow Jesus?

- What does Jesus say our responses should be to persecution? What does it mean that your reward is in heaven? How would faith be strengthened in times of trial? If you have faced times of trial, has your faith been strengthened?

- Why do Christians need a local church? Do you have a local church community? Do you have Christian friends? Do these relationships provide prayer and encouragement? Do you see your faith grow because of those friendships? How can your friendship strengthen other people's faith?

- What does it mean that Jesus has overcome the world? How does that provide comfort? Do you feel the difficulty of persecution? How can we (your parents) help you?

THE THIRD FLOOR

Biblical Truths

- Christians believe that God's word is *inerrant* (contains no errors), *authoritative* (obligates us to obey), and *sufficient* (provides wisdom for Christian living). The hostility and persecution we face as Christians flows from the convictions and beliefs of God's word (2 Tim. 3:16–17).

- Christians are called to be immovable in faith. We cannot pick what we believe or obey without damaging the integrity of Christian doctrine. Doctrine and ethics are a package deal. We must develop full resolve and courage, and we must not be swayed based on what is popular with the world (1 Cor. 15:58).

- Jesus tells us that we will face persecution. His apostles, Christians all through history, and other believers around the world today have faced and are facing serious persecution. Jesus said, "If the world hates you, know that it has hated me before it hated you. If you were of the world, the world would love you as its own; but because you are not of the world, but I chose you out of the world, therefore the world hates you" (John 15:18–19).

- It doesn't make sense to the world, but it is an honor to Christians to be persecuted and share in the sufferings of Christ. It deepens our faith and dependence upon him. We consider it a spiritual blessing to allow the Holy Spirit to guide us in times of trial and desperation, and we look for the sanctification and change in our hearts (Matt. 5:11–12).

- Christians need community and close friendship to face the challenges of persecution, testing, and trials of the world. Most of the relationships that we need, we find in our local churches. As you get ready to think about college or moving out of your parents' house, don't neglect the need for you to find and plug into a local church. You need friends who will have your back, pray for you, and affirm your faith as you stand firm against the world (James 5:16).

- Don't let persecution from the world stop you from sharing the good news of the gospel. Remember that Jesus has the victory! Jesus has already overcome the world (John 16:33)!

Conversation Starters

- What do Christians believe about God's word? What do *inerrant*, *authoritative*, and *sufficient* mean? Why does the world show Christians hostility and persecution? Do you believe these things about God's word?

- What is *faith*? What does it mean to be immovable in our faith? Why can we not pick and choose what we believe? How would that damage the doctrine of Christianity? What does it mean to develop full resolve and courage? Do you think you have developed that? Will our faith ever be fully popular with the world? Why or why not?

- What is persecution? What kinds of persecution do Christians face around the world? What does John 15:18–19 mean? Have you ever faced any kind of persecution for your faith or Christian beliefs?

- What does it mean to share in the sufferings of Christ? How does persecution deepen our faith and become a spiritual blessing? How does the Spirit guide us through trials? How does persecution lead to sanctification? Do you have stories of deepening faith and sanctification through persecution and trials?

- Why is it so important for Christians to have close community and Christian friendship? How does a local church help fulfill that need? How will you find a local church when you are living on your own? As the time gets closer, work with your parents to think through the criteria necessary for finding a healthy church and how to get settled (attending weekly, joining a community group, serving, etc.). Do you have friends who are able to help you be accountable and honest? Do you have friends who pray with you and for you? Do you have friends who affirm and agree with God's word and your faith? Do you have friends who help you stand firm against the world or who encourage you to make compromises? What sort of friend are you for others?

- Have you ever shared the gospel with someone? Was that scary? Were you afraid of being persecuted for that? What does it mean that Jesus has the victory and has already overcome the world? How does that give you comfort? Do you feel the weight of persecution? How can we (your parents) help you?

RECOMMENDED RESOURCES

Bonhoeffer, Dietrich, *The Cost of Discipleship*. London: SCM Press, 1959.

Holland, Tom. *Dominion: How the Christian Revolution Remade the World*. New York: Basic Books, 2019.

Kreider, Alan. *The Patient Firmament of the Early Church: The Improbable Rise of Christianity in the Roman Empire*. Grand Rapids, MI: Baker Academic, 2016.

Colson, Chuck, Robert George, and Timothy George, "The Manhattan Declaration: A Call of Christian Conscience." November 20, 2009. Manhattandeclaration.org.

Ortlund, Dane. *Gentle and Lowly: The Heart of Christ for Sinners and Sufferers*. Wheaton, IL: Crossway, 2020.

Wax, Trevin. *The Thrill of Orthodoxy: Rediscovering the Adventure of Christian Faith*. Downers Grove, IL: InterVarsity, 2022.

Walker, Andrew T., ed. *Social Conservatism for the Common Good: A Protestant Engagement with Robert P. George*. Wheaton, IL: Crossway, 2023.

Conclusion

THERE'S NO SECRET TRICK to what we've written about in these pages: *you* must be the person responsible for discipling your child. That is the single most important truth we can emphasize. Embrace the awkwardness and run toward the battle being waged for your child's heart.

To conclude this book, we wanted to provide tactical, on-the-ground advice for how to move forward with your child in this culture.

First, faithful membership and engagement with a local church is absolutely essential. We do not live in a culture that supports our Christian convictions. And given the frailty of human nature, we're more prone to go with the herd than stick out of the crowd. We cannot stress enough how your identity should come ultimately from Christ and your fellowship be the most intimate with those who are Christians. The local church is the means by which God has appointed his gospel to go forward. Isolated Christians cut off from encouragement and accountability are prone to wander and drift in their faith. We need each other for mutual encouragement and support. So yes, Mom and Dad, this means your church's calendar is more important than your child's sports schedule. Discipleship does not falter first and foremost by our becoming heretics but by isolation and drift.

Second, biblical literacy is absolutely essential. Strong discipleship is not something that happens casually. It takes time, energy, and focus. Scripture is clear that we must tuck its truths deep into our hearts to meditate on. We need correction from God's word. This will only happen by gaining familiarity with Scripture. There are many Bible reading plans available that we could recommend. It does not matter how familiar you or your child might be with Scripture. We always need more familiarity not less. Biblical ignorance is rampant in many Christian circles. If we're going to have the right instinct to go to Scripture when we encounter something in the culture we need to know *where* to go. To start with, read one Proverb a day and then try to read one chapter from both the Old Testament and New Testament. Reading two to three chapters of the Bible is a great way to begin gaining familiarity with not only the individual stories of the Bible, but the whole master narrative. What's beautiful about Scripture is that when read properly, it's the only book written by lots of authors over many cultures and across a large span of time that tells *one* story: the story of God redeeming the world through his Son, Jesus Christ.

Third, as we said in the introduction, we can't discuss every topic that should be discussed with your child, but here's a helpful set of diagnostic questions that could help you think through issues as you're confronted with new challenges.

1. What does the Bible say about this topic? What does the culture say about this topic in contrast to Scripture?
2. How does the Bible call us to live in response to this topic?
3. Where might you or your child be tempted to believe that the world's understanding of this topic is more alluring or correct than what Scripture teaches?
4. How does the issue tear at or promote your neighbor's flourishing?
5. How are we called to live in response to what the Bible says about this topic?

Fourth, to stay on top of the rapid pace of culture change, it's important to know what resources are available to stay current. These aren't the only resources we'd recommend, but here are a few organizations and resources that we trust and know will help support Christians and Christian parents in understanding the world from a Christian worldview.

1. Albert Mohler's *The Briefing* podcast
2. Focus on the Family
3. The Colson Center for Christian Worldview
4. Family Research Council
5. Allie Beth Stuckey's *Relatable* podcast
6. The Ethics and Religious Liberty Commission
7. Mama Bear Apologetics, mamabearapologetics.com
8. WORLD Magazine and WORLD Opinions
9. Alliance Defending Freedom
10. Bruce Ware's *Big Truths for Young Hearts* (Wheaton, IL: Crossway, 2009)

Mom and Dad, we pray that this book offers just one little step forward in cultivating your child's heart so that you can have an answer when asked about the big challenges confronting your children.

General Index

abortion, 25–26, 79, 79n1; basic case against abortion, 28–29; biblical teachings on, 26–29; biblical, theological, and philosophical truths concerning, 29–30; conversation starters for, 31, 31–32, 33; first-floor biblical truths on, 30–31; second-floor biblical truths on, 31; third-floor biblical truths on, 32–33

androgyny, 53

Artificial Intelligence (AI), 108

biblical ethics, 74

biblical ignorance, 150

biblical inerrancy, 74, 75, 142, 143

biblical literacy, 150

biblical truths, 7–8

children, 69–70n1; floors defined, 6; as a gift from God, 8–9

Christianity, 11, 12, 23, 27, 82, 83, 123; authentic, 136; criticism of, 84; and the doctrine of human dignity, 98; influence of, 135

Christians, 1, 3, 14, 22, 39, 81; approach of toward technology, 112; are to be good citizens, 121–22, 123–24, 125, 126, 131; called to be immovable in faith, 137, 144; and the common good, 130; criticism of, 84; cultural issues for, 4; engagement of with a local church, 149; as faithful, 120; as isolated, 149–50; must not be hyperpartisan, 125; need for community and friendships, 142, 144–45; parenting literature, 8; practicing important virtues in political engagement, 124–25; and prudence, 130–31. *See also* hostility and persecution; parents

chromosomes, 103

compassion, for the psychologically vulnerable, 98

culture: changes in America, 135; definitions of "boys" and "girls," 57; difficulty of being a parent today, 2; rapid change, 1

pornography, 107–8
prudence, 130–31

redemption, 109
reproduction, 37–38, 52, 54, 59,
65–66, 74, 95–96, 99, 103
righteousness, 9, 110, 115, 116, 120,
122, 123–24, 138

Satan, 2
Scripture, 15, 26–27, 71, 85;
on homosexuality, 67–68;
grounds identity in God,
89; prohibits the unlawful
taking of human life, 27–29;
understanding the storyline
of, 98, 104
secularism, 82
sex/sexuality, 35–36; abstinence
from, 41–42; attraction, 45;
biblical teaching on, 36–40,
74; biblical, theological, and
philosophical truths on, 40–
42; confusion, 35; conversation
starters for, 43, 44, 46–47;
defining morality of, 41;
ethics, 40, 45, 54; first-floor
biblical truths on, 42; purity,
42, 47; second-floor biblical
truths on, 43; confusion, 35;
self-control, 41, 45; sin, 41–42,
47, 69, 76; third-floor biblical
truths on, 44–46

sin/sinners, 71–72, 75, 101, 103,
112, 114–15, 120; of children,
69–70n1; deceitfulness of,
36–37; sexual, 41–42, 47, 69,
76

technology, 107–8; biblical
teachings, 108–11; biblical,
theological, and philosophical truths on, 112; carelessness toward, 108; Christian
wisdom on, 109; conversa-
tion starters for, 113–14,
114–15, 116–17; first-floor
biblical truths on, 113; need
for discernment on, 110–11;
second-floor biblical truths
on, 114; third-floor biblical
truths on, 115–16
transgenderism, 93–94; biblical
teachings on, 94–99; biblical,
theological, and philosophical
truths on, 99–100; conversation starters for, 100–1, 101–2,
104–6; first-floor biblical
truths on, 100; second-floor
biblical truths on, 101; third-
floor biblical truths on, 102–4
word of God, 2, 4, 150; as authoritative, 142, 143; as inerrant,
74, 75, 142, 143; as sufficient,
142, 143

Scripture Index